FAITH, FREEDOM, AND
THE FUTURE

FAITH, FREEDOM, AND THE FUTURE

BY

PETER TAYLOR FORSYTH
M.A., D.D.

Wipf & Stock
PUBLISHERS
Eugene, Oregon

Wipf and Stock Publishers
199 West 8th Avenue, Suite 3
Eugene, Oregon 97401

Faith, Freedom and the Future
By Forsyth, P.T.
ISBN: 1-57910-018-X
Publication date 12/5/1996

TO
LADY SPICER

PREFACE

THE dispute between the spirit and the letter is
one that has now burned itself out. As the area
of spiritual culture spreads, the worship of the
letter retires ; and everywhere now, it may be said,
the letter is recognised as the servant of the spirit—
to an extent even which often makes it its victim.
Not only is the letter made to yield the spirit's
larger interpretation, but it may even be erased as
an interpolation when it comes into collision with
the dogmatism of a ruling idea. Spirit has so
conquered all along the line that it is in danger
of losing some of the caution and consideration
which the victor can never safely discard. While
the letter stood in honour there seemed to be
something fixed, something in control of spiritual
vagrancy. But with its defeat the plea of spirituality may be made to cover anything from inspiration to eccentricity ; and even those who groaned
under the tyranny of the letter begin to wonder
if it was really worse than to be the sport of stray

lights and chance desires. The very 'spirit of Christ' may be used to dissolve His historic existence, and the rich development of revelation to rob it of all finality.

So that the issue which now confronts us, if we are not to keep slaying the slain, is not that of the letter and the spirit; but it is the question where, in the victory of spirit, room is to be found for any control at all, or place for any norm of the spiritual life. Where is our last resort—to *Authority* or *Subjectivity*? For the hour civilisation is the victim of subjectivity. Some one said lately that the present age is the most conceited of all ages. At least it is the most full of its own subjectivity. It is true that social trouble or social omen is rousing some fear, and leading people to ask if our subjective liberty and sufficiency is really able to carry itself. But it will take a long time for the misgivings to get as deep as the confidence. And meantime it is an evil time for the seers who face the crowd with a real claim for a veritable and royal Word of the Lord.

To take the familiar case which is suggested by such a phrase—the case of the Bible. What is its place still in Christianity? We certainly cannot treat it as the Reformers did ; nor is the warfare round it parallel to that which raged between them and the critics of their day. It cannot be, since the result of the conflict to which I have alluded between the letter and the spirit. The religion of the Reformation can never more be staked on the integrity of the letter of Scripture. Critical science has changed all that. But the question remains all the same. If the letter of Scripture is not final, is there anything in Scripture that is ? Is there anything authoritative in the Bible ? Is all its interpretation at the mercy of subjective impression ? If we have settled the issue between letter and spirit, have we not still to face the question between Word and Spirit ? Is there a Word in the Bible for ever to which all the rest of the book is but an aura ? Is there in the Bible, still and for ever, a Gospel which is the one guarantee of both certainty and freedom, which is the creator of all freedom and the liberty in all certainty ? Has the Bible a finality in it, or is the finality the light which lighteth every man in the world ? Is the core of the Bible something definitive and normative for ever, or has the book only a function instrumental and suggestive ? Does the soul there find a new creation ; or is the Bible but the means of stimulating and evoking the native resources of the soul at its best ? Is the Christ of the Bible the Redeemer or the Symbol of Humanity ?

It is not a new issue. It is one that is most keenly felt indeed in the Churches that are known as the Free Churches ; but just because they are Churches it is not confined to them, but it is active wherever there is real life in any Church. It ought to be viewed in that great context of a whole Church facing the whole world. Its historic bearings ought to be taken. And the Free Churches especially ought to realise that it is an old legacy for them, and indeed an original entail. For English Dissent did not arise out of the Reformation directly or alone. It arose equally out of the dissenters of the Reformation—the Anabaptists, or however they may be called. And the great issue between the Reformers and the Anabaptists was that which rages so keenly now. It was the issue between a final Word and a free Spirit.

It is the object of these pages, published in the two hundred and fiftieth anniversary of the creation of Nonconformity by the Act of Uniformity, to trace this issue through this parentage and legacy in the particular case of the community of the author's birth and nurture; his fatherland, and never his mere platform; to which his love and service have been paid, always under a ruling allegiance to the great and true Church of Christ whereof it is a part. We are only now beginning to feel the practical meaning of many of our favourite ideas about the Church and the democracy. Our loose phrases are being translated into serious action. And it is well to ask what history has to say upon the subject—our own history in particular. If we treated history right (supposing we knew it) one half of our own problems would vanish, and we should have the key of the other. It may be, also, that the discussion of the large question in the case of a single branch of the Church may have some value for the rest. For the writer's eye is always on the Church Universal, the world of men, and the Saviour of the race.

There never was so much public interest bestowed on Christ as to-day. And it takes two forms in chief—when it assumes public dimensions at all. Christ is regarded as central by all who regard Him in a serious way. But central to what? One

class of mind sees the whole cosmic issue condensed in human history, all history centred in
that of the soul, and the grand symbol of the soul
and its meaning set forth for our reverence in
Christ. Christ is the spiritual centre of a system
of things which is spiritual at last or nothing. He
is the grand register of man's confidence in his
own spiritual destiny and his power to realise it,
the chief symbol in a long history which can offer
the soul no more than symbols of itself. The
symbolism of rites becomes in Him the symbolism
of personality. He is the great illustration of
truths and ideas which must always shine by their
own light, and guarantee to an intuition their own
power and permanence.

   But another class of mind does not begin with
the cosmic problem, even as history, nor with ideas
self-luminous and self-sufficient. It begins with
the moral problem—of course on a historic scale.
It begins with the purpose of God, the Word of
God, and man's historic treatment of it. It begins
not with the problem of history, but with the
revelation in history, not with a problem that
revelation may solve, but with a crisis that revelation creates. Its problem is not Adversity but

Guilt. It starts with Christ, not as the Symbol of man's aspiration, or the Hero of his resource, but as the Incarnation of God's purpose, or at least the Prophet of God's will. He is the centre of a system of Grace and Sin.

For the one class Christ is the centre of spiritual Humanity; for the other He is the centre of the will and grace of God.

It is the writer's view that the latter is the New Testament Christ, the Christ Eternal.

But it is not as if the two positions faced each other irreconcilably. For the latter includes the former. The dogmatic Christ is the only key to great history, the only warrant of its great destiny. The Christ of revelation alone realises all the great aspiration and destiny of man for which the historic figure to many stands as but symbol. The deed done in Christ alone realises for ever the ideas crystallised in Christ. And He is the centre of any scheme of the world as ideal history only because He is the centre and substance of God's grace to actual sinful history. Christ we cannot evade, either as humanists or as theologians. Nor can we evade His centrality. But we can and must choose whether He is the transfiguration of spiritual

Humanity, with its eternal destiny still unsure as a great surmise; or whether He is the foregone achievement of that destiny, as the incarnation of God's will of grace for the creation of the New Humanity. Is He man's spiritual ideal projected and cherished, or man's eternal consummation presented and guaranteed ? Is He there for our admiration as our highest self, or for our appropriation as God's highest boon ?

The conviction in which the writer lives is that it is only the latter view of Christ that gives any permanent value to the former; that Christ is no revelation of a glorious Humanity except as He is the incarnation and agent of God's purpose and act with a Sinful Humanity; that He is no splendid creature, but the New Humanity's holy Creator.

All that is said in this little book is said as one particular application of this supreme text—its illustration in the genesis and genius of Independency viewed as a factor in the great Church and history of the West.

CONTENTS

LECTURE I

THE WORD AND THE SPIRIT [1]

IT is in remarkable contrast with the manner of our own time that in the New Testament we find little said about spirituality and much about the Holy Ghost. To-day we seem to have in some cases not so much as heard of a Holy Ghost. Certain Christian types have practically erased that element from their belief, and they do not appear to feel the poorer; whereas spirituality—they seek and ensue it. They set little store by positive belief if they but discern this note. Any truth is true enough which goes with this temper. Believe as you will if only you show the spirit of Christ. The spirit of Christ is not a creative power which leads into all truth but a responsive

[1] May I explain on the threshold what will often recur, that when I speak of the Word here I do not identify it with the Bible, with the Canon. The Word is man's responsive and inspired act of confessing the Gospel as the new creative act of God. It took effect first in the Apostles, and then in the continuous and manifold publication of their message by the Church. And by the Spirit is meant not simply God's presence in the world He made, nor even His presence in History by the historic Son and His posthumous effect, but God's presence in the Church in an Eternal Son and a *Holy* Spirit Who not only fills the Word but mediates it to the soul.

A

mood, a frame of mind which cultivates much dogmatic indifference, that is, carelessness of truth. Religion is love and not faith. It is a state, and not an act or a judgment. Hence, as M. Faguet says, it tends to shirk responsibility in action and to court incompetence in belief. To use philosophic language, the subjectivity of the age feels itself comparatively independent of objective reality, and especially of historic. A carelessness of facts, passing into chronic slipshod and habitual unveracity, grows up upon the spiritualist mind. Such a case as the Jatho case in Germany shows, by the passionate popularity of a nebulous but devout and amiable man whom his national church has called to order, that, in the mind of many, truth has little to do with a church compared with temperament, and faith little compared with the idealism of an agreeable religiosity. To put it briefly, the Spirit is detached more or less completely from the Word. History becomes as indifferent as doctrine. And we are at one of these gnostic crises that tend continually to recur in the Church's history, where we are not only urged to the conversion of the good, but this regeneration of the regenerate is believed to be effected by a second and inward revelation which does not develop the historic first but supersedes it. The age, the Church, has another comforter than the Jesus who promised

Him by saying, ' I will come unto you ' (John xiv. 16 ; cp. 18). It is on this matter of the relation of the Gospel Word and the Holy Spirit that I would first speak, as the foundation of the history I propose to discuss. It would be a history of the Church of vast value which should be written from this point of view—the progressive contact or collision of the Word and the Spirit.

One cannot write for general reading on these subjects without a haunting sense of some hostility from parts of the public that one would expect rather to interest. There are those who will say, we are ready to hear about history, and about religion in history, but let it be the story of heroes, saints, or martyrs. Both history and religion are personal things. Let us be told, if you will, how great the struggle of ages has been for the simple faith the plain man understands. But why obtrude into the history of such a religion as Christ's the discussion of subtle differences, or make it, as it has too often been made, the arena of theological dispute ? When you begin by asking us to distinguish spirituality from the Holy Spirit, and modern subjectivity from the objective religion of the Old Testament, when you try to show the action in history of such refinements as these, are you not doing what the theologians have too often done,

and importing scholastic hairsplitting into great
affairs ?

One cannot but feel much sympathy with the
lay mind in the subtle stage at which religious
questions have arrived in an hour like the present.
It feels confronted with issues of which no account
was taken either in the traditional Biblicism of its
upbringing or in the general quality of its education.   The old discussions go on in a new language,
with a new set of ideas, which bewilder and irritate
the mind trained to believe that plain honesty
should settle everything, and that the jury should
always snub the expert.   The attitude in religious
matters corresponds here to that in social, where
an utterly new temper, outlook, and method on
the part of Labour exasperates Capital with a sense
of helplessness and nameless peril.   One cannot but
feel some sympathy for the honest and forthright
person who dismisses discussion, calls a plague on
both your houses, discards the theologians as
faddists, hobbyists, and gratuitous sophisticators,
refuses their guidance, and either closes down upon
the ultimatum of a text or two, or cherishes a
doctrinal Agnosticism on a pathless moor of liberty
in a warm mist of charity.

And truly if one threw into the halfpenny daily
press discussions on the metaphysics of Godhead,

after the manner in which they pervaded the market-places of the fourth century, one would deserve the charge of gratuitous pedantry. But it is quite another thing that is done when, on the great survey of religious history, people are asked to mark the action of vast experimental principles which can also be condensed into doctrines. We are then dealing not with metaphysical religion but with psychological, with the Spirit's action in experience. To read the history of the Church thus is to read the spiritual autobiography of the race. Now every man who comes to maturity or age with a soul history and the power still to think knows, when he looks back, how different the course of his life has been from what it would have been if it had been made only by the intentions, ambitions, and purposes on which he was most conscious and most keen. He recognises that these plans, these ideals, have been largely thwarted or disappointed, and in any case overruled; and he is what he is in virtue of other guidance than his own, and other powers and ideas than those on which he put his direct and fervent pressure. He either owns the guiding hand of a wise God, or, if he cannot rise so high, he perceives the action of ideas and principles turning him in a long curve, and moulding him with a slow, often unfelt, always irresistible pressure. They permeate life, where his own purposes only bestrode it.   And he stands, not where he proposed to do, but where they have brought him—so far at least as that inward man is concerned, which is the truly real, and which he alone sees, however dimly.

It is not otherwise with the race and the history of its soul.   ' In the unreasoning progress of the world a wiser Spirit is at work than ours,' a Spirit not simply mightier but wiser, a Spirit whose insight is such that it has sometimes staked the whole human career upon issues which to all men at the time, and not only to the fumbling plain man, seemed a gratuitous refinement of thought, or a quixotic fantasy of conscience.   At *the* most crucial hour of the world's history they all forsook Him and fled.   He saw issues to be prime and eternal which to all other men were either not understood or, in so far as they were, seemed forced and over fine.   He inverted the perspective of current values.[1]   And at this very

---

[1] Compare Browning's risen Lazarus in *Karshish* :—

> ' The man is witless of the size, the sum,
> The value in proportion of all things,
> Or whether it be little or be much.
> Discourse to him of prodigious armaments
> Assembled to besiege his city now,
> And of the passing of a mule with gourds—
> 'Tis one !   Then take it on the other side,
> Speak of some trifling fact—he will gaze rapt
> With stupor at its very littleness
> (Far as I see) as if in that indeed

hour the issues which will really determine the Church's future are those most hidden from the wise and prudent in affairs, even religious affairs ; who are irritated that such subtleties should be thrust on their common-sense, full time, and taxed minds. And the resentment is especially keen where religion is held to be a means of comfort or enjoyment, never designed to make our decent pleasures less, or disturb the immunities of nescience.

In the following pages I shall be a good deal occupied with one distinction on which may be said to turn the whole course of the Church's history, and much of its contact with the world. I mean the distinction, and the relation, between the Word and the Spirit, between a religion of fact and a religion of conscience, between Christianity as the religion of the historic final Word and Christianity as the

> He caught prodigious import, whole results,
> And so will turn to us the bystanders
> In ever the same stupor (note this point)
> That we too see not with his opened eyes.
> Wonder and doubt come wrongly into play,
> Preposterously at cross purposes.
> Should his child sicken unto death—why, look
> For scarce abatement of his cheerfulness ;
> While a word, gesture, glance from that same child
> At play, or in the school, or laid asleep,
> Will startle him to an agony of fear,
> Exasperated, just as like.'

religion of the living and moving Spirit.   I shall
have to urge how real is the distinction, and how
vital the connection, between these in all that
pertains to the salvation committed to the Church;
and to trace how their approximation or their
departure colours whole ages, movements, and
churches; how their interaction, so powerful at the
very beginning, is equally potent to-day.   I wish
especially to illustrate these two elements in connection with the origin and nature of English
Independency, as leading to modern Democracy,
and to show how its greatest life depends on
their reality and true relation.   And if to
any the interest fails in such study, and they
prefer the purely biographical, heroic, and impressionist treatment of religious history, I am
afraid I must lose attention which I would much
rather keep and carry with me.   But what we need
at the moment is the power to understand the
time as the condition of guiding it.   It is not
ardours but intelligence, not trumpets but maps,
an understanding both of our Gospel and our age.
To force theology on history is an undertaking
which experience shows to be calamitous where it
is not absurd.   To force it even on the Church,
where it is essential, is not wise or prudent.   But
to show that God theologises in the history of the
Church, as He certainly did in its creation, and

to show that the history of the world is groaning and travailing with the mystery of those ideas which in the Church are manifest doctrine—that is something very different. To read the ways of God in Christ out of history is a very different thing from inventing them and forcing them into it. And to be led to see that they are there is an essential part of our equipment for the service of any church which exists to effect God's thought and purpose with history, and not merely to realise certain humane ideals.

The new religion of Christianity was not based solely upon the verdict of the spiritual consciousness but on the interaction of two sets of facts : first, the life, miracles, teachings, death, and resurrection of Jesus ; and second, the action of the Holy Spirit upon the living generation. The former was valuable only as interpreted and appropriated in the latter. The resurrection of Christ, for instance, as it took place by the Spirit, so had its meaning only by the same Spirit. The world was as alien to the idea of Christ's resurrection as to the spiritual experiences in its wake. But the Christian certainty rested on the indwelling of the same eternal Spirit by Whom Christ offered Himself and was raised from the dead.

But the higher we rise in the scale of truth so

much the more subtle and seductive become the
possibilities of error, and the more serious error
becomes, not, perhaps, for the individual, but for the
Church and its future.   And here was a danger—the
danger of the Spirit's becoming detached from the
Word, and the Church's experience escaping from
its creative facts.   This soon took place in Gnosticism, against whose beginnings the whole of the
later part of the New Testament is a protest.
And the first step in the process was the allegorising
of the facts, and their employment for homiletic
rather than evangelical use.   They were treated as
symbols, and not as creative acts of God.   They
became indifferent as creative facts, and valuable
only as edifying suggestions, or as expressions of
spiritual experiences which, however much they
owed to the facts as stimuli, could, once they were
started, go on without them.   The historic fact
became subordinated to the spiritual experience
as its mere parable or its suggestion, and finally
it was denied and treated as lumber.

   This is a course which has been frequently
repeated in one form or another in the Church's
history; and, in one form or another, it has
always to be arrested, and to be forced back on
the facts—though never without being overruled
for gain in the long-run both to the Word and the
Spirit.

We have therefore in the New Testament, at the very beginning of the Church, the two elements of the Word and the Spirit, evangelism and spiritualism, the historic and the pneumatic. Both were quite necessary for the missionary action of the Church, as we see from Peter's evangelical interpretation of the tongues in Acts ii. And when John xvi. 13 says of the Spirit, ' He shall not speak of Himself, but whatsoever He shall hear that shall He speak,' we have the same inseparable connection expressed in the form of a justification of the fourth Gospel in relation to the Synoptics. The ministry of the Spirit was not to supersede the historic salvation, and yet it was to do more than merely transmit it. It was to be at once its continuity, its amplification, and its individualisation—all three. The Holy Spirit was never to be detached from the fontal Word. Nothing is more certain than this in the New Testament. Any manual of New Testament theology will illustrate textually the fact that Word and Spirit are, if not identical, yet inseparable aspects of one power and one action. Things done in one place by the Word—things like conversion or regeneration— are done in another by the Spirit.

We can further mark the process by which the Church was led, from speaking of the unique thing in Christ as the Spirit which moved the prophets, to recognising it as distinct from that by a difference more than gradual. It was not merely the same Spirit acting in another way—it was now something more intimately divine, the Holy Spirit. The Spirit *visited* the prophets, they *had* the Spirit ; but Christ, the living Word, *was identified* with Him, with not only the power but the holiness of God. When Paul in Romans i. 4 says that Christ rose by the spirit of holiness, the meaning of holiness there is not merely ethical. For in the Old Testament the Holy Spirit of God is more than that, and means the majesty and sublimity and Godhead of a God that transcends even the ethical world. The spirit of holiness which rose in Christ was the supernatural element which placed Him in the eternal majesty of God, and set Him as far above prophets or kings as these were above nature. We are here dealing not with the spirit of the Creator uniquely pervading the creation, nor only with the unique presence of God in human history, selecting a nation or inspiring its prophets, or living in a Son, but with His unique and individual action in the Church of the Son's regenerates—with the Holy Spirit. The Holy Spirit is associated in the most close and exclusive way with the act of the Son, the action of the Word, and the existence of a Church of new souls. It is given by Christ as

His greatest gift; therefore it was the fruit of His greatest act and consummation. It has its source in the Cross, and its first action in the Resurrection and its Word. Its prime action therefore is in its nature miraculous; it is not to ethicise, not to sanctify, but first to regenerate, by organising men into Christ's new creation. So that it is not one of Christ's gifts, as the Gospel is not, but the complete and effective gift of Christ Himself, as the Saviour of the world brought home to the individual in the communion of God and the community of a Church. So that, also, we cannot continue to speak of the Spirit as *it*, but must go on to speak of *Him*, as He enters more deeply the personal life.

The Holy Spirit is thus inseparable from this work of Christ and from the word of it in the apostolic preaching which is crystallised in the Bible. It is certainly not, in the New Testament, the Christlike spirit, meaning thereby a particular type of religious subjectivity, a specific frame of mind. In the New Testament the Holy Spirit, the Lord the Spirit, is an objective power, working, before all sanctification, a new creation, and effecting it from the focal point of the Cross and Resurrection, and the thing done there once for all. It is not the spirit of discipleship but of regeneration by that Word. The suggestion is not

approaching an ideal but crossing a Rubicon.
And it creates not a fraternity but a Church.
God's action in the Spirit is thus not an independent action alongside the Word, or following
it and crowning it.   It is not as if a first act of God
gave historical information in the general Word,
and a second fructified it for particular experience.
We have not two causalities.   Such an idea cuts
the certainty from faith in the Word.   It lands
us in an idea of absolute predestination, apart
from the Gospel, on the one hand, or in a false
and unhistoric mysticism on the other.   There is
an inner and organic connection between the
Word and the Spirit.   It is not partnership, it
is wedlock, not co-operation but polarity.   For the
purposes of salvation the Spirit acts reciprocally in,
with, and through the Word, as in the natural
realm God does through nature.   The Holy Spirit
does not effect a direct contact of God as the
spiritual power with man's inner nature, as if it
switched on the inner light.   That makes the
work of Christ either superfluous or no different
in kind from the work of all other men in
rousing and kindling nature.   And it could not
then be the supreme and distinguishing act of
God's love, as it is so constantly called in the
New Testament (John iii. 16, Romans viii. 32).
Revelation would then be but illumination, and

not redemption; it would flood us and submerge, rather than lift and save. The response would be but visionist and not moral, it would be but insight not committal, knowledge not action, piety not faith, states and feelings and not will, turning on a truth we perceive rather than a reality we enter. The Word is the organ of the Holy Spirit for the purposes of salvation into holiness. And yet not in the sense that the Spirit inspired the Word and then left it to act for itself, as the Deists used to think God made the world, and retired from it, and left it to run. The Holy Spirit which inspired the universal Word is not only immanent in it always as the Creator Spirit is in universal nature, but also present to the soul every time the Word comes home. The ministry of the Word is the chief agency of the Holy Ghost, and the chief function of the Church; whose business is not simply publication of a truth but confession of an experience—the experience of the indwelling Spirit as its life. It is the Holy Spirit that makes the Word to be revelation; it is the Word that makes revelation historic and concrete. It is historic not only in the sense of being actual, but in the sense of being concrete with history, solidary with the organic whole of historic affairs, and not merely pointed for illuminate individuals, or diffused in mystic humanity. The action of the Spirit

through the historic Word is integral to God's
whole action on the race.   There is no action of
God on man which is out of relation to his central,
final, and saving action in Christ by the power of
the Holy Ghost.   Light from God comes indeed
to man without the historic mediation of Christ.
But it is all from the God and Father of Christ.
And in Christ alone is the power of God unto the
race's salvation, and so to its final illumination.

In contrast with all this is the spiritualist position.   Its chief features are, first, its attempt at
direct contact with God and its rejection of the
idea of mediation, even by Christ; second, its claim
to have a new knowledge of God, a real addition to
historic revelation, to have a revelation which is not
a deeper realisation of the old but a new communication ; and, third, a great lack of clearness, steadi-
ness, and certainty beyond the moment.   It seeks
the final and certain revelation of God in an inner
witness He bears of Himself in men's souls.   This
alone gives freedom from all external authority,
including that of the historic past and its figures.
This alone seems direct intercourse with God,
and to its bar Christ Himself must be brought.
There is by comparison no external and historic
Word, none with finality, none *within which* all
personal illumination in spiritual things moves but

as its explication. Historical revelation is but initial preparation. It is an early stage, substantially outgrown. We do not meet God in a historic Christ made present by the Spirit, but in a spirit once symbolised in the historic Christ. The only locus of revelation is the individual experience (Christ being but a particular case of it); whose culmination is in passive impressions, convictions, perceptions, visions, ecstasies, or suchlike forms of direct illumination by the inner light or ' the ideal Christ.' Revelation means only direct communication by God to individuals in moments of exaltation or insight which may supersede history. The spirit becomes a second, and higher, and ultimate revelation, whether received as a supernatural action, or taken as the natural spirituality of man at his best. Such is natural as distinct from Christian mysticism, whether enthusiastic or speculative.

There are in the New Testament no more than points of attachment for such a view; but they seemed to give footing to movements in Church history which discarded the finality and sufficiency of the Word—movements like Montanism, Gnosticism, Mysticism, and Anabaptism. Repressed by the Reformation the tendency flamed up again in Pietism. And it was reinforced by speculative philosophy, which revived the old Gnosticism by

its doctrine of the self-explication of the infinite
Spirit overruling all historic testimony, and emerging to a progressive self-realisation in the phenomena
of history and the soul. The career of spiritualism,
thus cut off from historic finality, ends in Rationalism
(as our own day freely shows), wherein the natural
knowledge of God is made the key to the Gospel,
instead of the Gospel becoming the key to it.

Of course such spiritualisms have their place and
use. Negatively they have been provoked as protests
by the hardening up of religious truth, by the mere
theologising of the Word of God, and its precipitation
into a system with its appeal to the understanding.
And their protest has been of great value, especially
for individuals. But they cannot be permanent.
And they cannot found or sustain a society, a
church. They rest too much upon impressions,
temperamental, momentary, and open to challenge
in a more sober light. They do not come for good,
like a historic revelation spiritually discerned. An
imagined Christ does not stay like a historic who
is also eternal. They breed a religion moodish
rather than personal, whereas in the Gospel we have
personal communion with Christ in all life's functions, and not simply in its mystic moments. The
speculative substitution even of an immanent
Logos-Christ for the historic, or for the mystic,
does not give a fixed point of certainty for the

generations, any more than the more exaltées moments do for the individual. No spiritualism can give us a fixed point for practical certainty if it finds the Word of the historic Gospel to be a limitation, instead of that one sacrament, release, and opening of all things which it is for faith.

In the New Testament then we have two orders, two factors, of spiritual power working together, which have also continued to interact through the whole course of the Church's history, and have moulded it according to the predominance of each. They are the Word and the Spirit, the Bible and the Church, the historic element and the pneumatic, evangelism and spiritualism. If we contrast them, the one turns on the historic Word in its finality and normality from the past, the other on the co-ordination with it of a present life and experience. The one is concerned with a mighty record, the other with a mighty power and life. The one furnishes the element of fixity and continuity, the other of movement and variety. The one, the Word, like a thunder sound, is communal to the whole Church, the other, like a voice, is specialised for the soul. The one is apostolic, in that it is the experimental witness once for all of men with a unique charge from Christ ; the other is prophetic, in being the witness of souls who have simply a vivid spiritual

experience, but not necessarily *that* experience, the
experience of the apostolic fact.   The one produces
regenerates by the gift of grace, the other tends to
produce illuminates, charismatics, or even eccentrics, with special gifts that need the Word's control.
The one makes believers, the other saints or adepts.
The one is deliberate, ordered, weighty, and sure,
the other enthusiastic, rhapsodic, or even orgiastic ;
the one a church, the other a synagogue of the
Libertines.   The one works by the intuition of the
fact, the other by the intuition of the soul.   The
one made the base of the Church, the other deployed
it.   The young Church had early to secure its base of
fact against a free spirituality more dangerous than
sheer paganism ; and it did so in the rule of faith, in
creed, canon, and episcopate, which were its stay in
an age swept by pneumatic excitement both within
the Church and without.   And the Church, organised on this base, though it did sometimes quell
the pneumatic enthusiasm, in the main harnessed
it for its work in the world, as the great spiritual
organiser, Paul, did with his Corinthians and their
tongues (1 Cor. xiv.).   It was a control that was
met with much recalcitrance, even when the
authority was that of an apostle, as we see from
Eph. iv. 14, where he has not pagans but Christians
in his eye.   And had the authority of the apostles
with their creative facts failed, the young Church

THE WORD AND THE SPIRIT 21

would have dissolved in spiritual anarchy and
futility. But in deploying the spiritual resources
of the Church this control was not wanting.

A sketch of Church history, written from this
point of view by the skilled pen of a competent
scholar with the seeing eye and the understanding
heart, would be a great service to the Christian
public to-day. The point of view I mean is the
contact, the friction, the reciprocity of the Word
and the Spirit, of the official and the evangelical, of the institutional and the enthusiastic, of
tradition and spontaneity; and of these not in a
banal antithesis of death and life, but as living and
powerful on both sides. Nothing would make it so
clear how little novelty there is in much modernism;
how venerable the new theologies are; how much respect their antiquity deserves; how perennial is their
principle, how varied its form; how the Gospel in
the first few centuries broke the back of that
principle for good; how its fragments enriched the
Gospel whose life it threatened by its integrity;
what a tonic the Gnostic or critical principle may
be on the one hand, or the mystic on the other, to
a sound historical constitution to which it would be
fatal as a life; how richly speculation may exploit
a faith it cannot create; how it may serve and adorn
in harness a church which it would wreck if it drove.

And the most interesting chapter, perhaps, of such a book would show us the play, within even the first century and the New Testament, of almost every principle or idea that distracts or threatens a church of the Gospel to-day. Apostolic Christianity did not make itself good in a mental vacuum, but it was secured in direct conflict with the principle of every heresy that has threatened its life from then till now. Protestantism has perhaps been unduly engrossed by the struggle of St. Paul with Judaism ; and it is but awaking to the significance of other and more pagan conflicts, which he began by facing in Thessalonians and Corinthians, which returned to engage his later years, which engrossed St. John, so that it is only by their knowledge that we can understand his Epistles, and which in the temporary retreat of Paulinism (then as now) held the field.

Such a chapter would have to point out that even in the New Testament we can see many members of the Church parting from it, not in a frank relapse to the world, but in the foundation of rival churches with the same Christian name but another liberty than Christ's. We can see men who were brought in by the apostolic preaching starting to missionise on their own account with fresh revelationary capital, founding on visionary experiences, outgrowing the Word in what they held

to be the power of the Spirit, holding themselves to
be vessels of the Spirit more than the antiquated
apostles were, cultivating a more rapt and mystic
religion, and construing Christianity on the more
liberal creed of gnosis rather than grace, of thought
rather than faith, of intuition rather than history.
They impressed people by a magnetism, a facility,
and a confidence which the apostles, much humbled
and scarcely saved, did not command. They
offered a liberty very different from that wherewith
Christ made apostles free. To their ardours, at
their height, everything was lawful ; and therefore
sin was mostly a fiction. It could certainly be
made too much of. They lowered and practically
erased the fence between the Church and the age,
and adjusted the Cross with so much ingenuity to
the culture and comfort of the hour that it also
was erased from their gospel. This brought them
into a contrast with the faithful Church which rose
to antagonism ; and love of the household of faith
was changed to hate for official Christianity and
a gospel to the conscience. The historic Jesus was
submerged or evaporated in the atmosphere of
the Spirit. Or He became a mere symbol of God,
with a fleeting significance as history outgrew
Him, with no resurrection, no reality, and no
return. His cross became but a symbol of cosmic
or spiritual process. The churches of St. Paul

and St. John were troubled with libertinism, with
the visionism of people who claimed superior en-
lightenment as pneumatics and prophets, with
Gnosticism which served up the Gospel as rational
truth dressed with sentimental jelly, and treated
the resurrection of Christ either as a myth they
had outgrown or as an ideal process in whose midst
they all were.

And there were many who fell in with the ways
of pagan society, only bringing to them a certain
religious aspiration and refinement which even
paganism could not command. Throughout it all
the death of Christ was pushed into a corner, like
an embarrassing episode of which the less said the
better. And throughout all also ran one philosophic
principle as coherent at bottom as the unity of the
jealous God and Gospel it opposed. Insight took
the place of faith and claimed a higher measure
of the Spirit, a purer knowledge of God and His
wisdom. It tended to banish repentance from its
experience, as spiritual culture always does when
it claims to outgrow evangelical faith. The fear
of God dropped to a crude and inferior stage of
religion. The idea of discipline vanished from
church life ; and an extravagant idea of personal
liberty, imported from the natural democracy,
took the first place, vacated by the obedience of
faith. They readily formed groups which were

first irritant within the Church and then rivals
without. Where they did not move towards
libertinage they took to the other extreme of
ascetic and gratuitous abstinence. Emancipation
took the place of redemption, and revolution of
regeneration.

These tendencies spread through the more
cultivated churches of Asia Minor, carried by
wandering evangelists of much spiritual claim,
who urged the distinction of the earthly Jesus
and the heavenly Christ, and sought by their culture of a spiritual Christ to deliver the soul from
the bondage of a historic Saviour. The keen theological conflict of the next century or two only
carried the same issues into a larger field ; and the
Athanasian victory, which saved Christianity for
Europe and Europe for the future, was at bottom
no more than a repetition, on the scale of a great
church, of the apostolic victory gained on the New
Testament area for all time.

Certainly the duty and the blessing of each age
is to handle the perennial opponent of the Gospel
in the form in which the age presents it. We have
both to surmount and to utilise the Gnosticism of
to-day as truly as the Church of the first centuries
did with the form that faced it. But it is very
much gained for the quietness and confidence of our
strength to know that it is no strange trial of faith

that befalls us, that it is in principle the same antagonist still, with the same signature of defeat upon him, and the same possibilities in him to be our mighty helper when he has been reduced to the service of a faith he once thought to command.   It is easy for the untaught to think that the challenge of to-day belongs to a departure of the twentieth century which at last is to make all things new.   And for public and social freedom how true it often is, and how hopeful.   And for the science of our faith and Gospel it has also much that is true and useful in it.   But for the fact and faith of the Gospel it is not true.   And a due knowledge of the past would teach us how little it is true.   And it would give us to feel that we are in a host which is always but following up, through a country deeply disaffected, a victory which has been won from a historic beginning, and has never to be gained again.

We have seen that the function of the Spirit in the Church was not simply to transmit the Word but to develop it.   And Newman's question soon arose : How far might this go ?   How shall we know what is development and what degeneration ? What is the note of a true tradition ?   How are we to distinguish the evolution of the Gospel fact from the evolution of a mere spiritual idea, the realisation of the old from the revelation of a

new ? How can we tell what is the development
of the old revelation and what is the invasion
of new ? Does the Spirit really extend the region
of revelation, or only continue, enrich, and in-
dividualise the original, sole, and compendious
revelation ? Is there a second and superior revelation of the Spirit which makes the first old ?

It was largely to meet this difficulty that both the
belief and life of the Church became more organised, and a canonical base was provided for the
Church in the Bible, where the present Spirit coin-
cided with a living Word. But control has been
hard to fix; and the enthusiasm of a spiritualism
beyond or without the Word has broken out vehe-
mently from time to time, as the Church overdid its
function and sterilised the Word. It made Gnosticism, Montanism, Mysticism, Anabaptism, and, to a
certain extent, the tradition of the Roman Church.

Spiritualism was either natural or supernatural.
It either fell back, with a Logos-idea, on the rational
spirit native to man at his best, inbreathed by the
Creator at the first, and unspoiled at the centre by
sorrow or sin, on a rational spirituality, which made
the speculative idealism of the Gnostic pneumatics.
Or, with the more apostolic pneumatics, it believed
in a supernatural invasion of that human nature by
the special action of God, by the Holy Ghost—only
a Holy Ghost that found a historic revelation to gall

it by its limitations, and that could only surmount them by superseding such a historic revelation, and treating it with the utmost freedom. This supernatural spiritualism, again, took two forms. One was represented by the tradition which the Roman Church made parallel to the Bible, rising outside apostolic sources, due to the visions or the judgment of individual saints or companies, and sometimes standing above the apostolic Bible, and continually tending to do so. Its true nature was expressed when Pio Nono said, 'I am tradition.' And its tendency is farther illustrated by the contrasted behaviour of Luther and of Loyola when each was in spiritual despair at the crisis of his life. Luther, in a true apostolic succession, turned to the Bible, Loyola betook himself to visions and such direct dealings with the spiritual world. The one found refuge in the Word with the Spirit, the other in the Spirit without the Word.[1] The other form of supernatural spiritualism is represented by Montanism and Anabaptism, and especially the latter, where the immediate inspiration took the reins from the historic Gospel, went round the Reformation and behind it, and found its point of attachment in the Roman Mysticisms which so attracted Luther at first, but from which he clearly emerged. Rome, Anabaptism, Modernism are all in one strain.

[1] It is not so wonderful at bottom that Jesuits become Modernists.

Its note is perpetual revelation, in the same sense
in which the Bible contains revelation; and revelation under individual conditions which tend to be
ecstatic, and irresponsible to either the written or
preached word. It dwells upon the prolongation
of Christ rather than His appropriation. It lives
in communities with an ethical rigour and an
ascetic simplicity, which is compounded for by
unlimited spiritual licence in the way either of
belief, or of feeling, of or prophecy. For the
Reformation, especially, in both its Swiss and
German forms, it made danger and damage which
threatened to undo the Gospel and restore the
kingdom to Rome. We shall see in Independency
how it affected the Reformation in its English form.

It has been said with much truth that in the
relation of Word and Spirit Spiritualism recognises
only the divine factor in salvation, Rationalism only
the human, Calvinism clearly distinguishes, and
even disjoins, them (though it always associates
them), and Lutheranism puts them in an organic
unity of constant mutual immanence and interaction. And here, perhaps, the Lutheran side is
deeper and nearer the truth. The action of the
Spirit is immediate to the soul yet not unmediated
by the Word. The Spirit when He had set the
Word down in history did not abdicate for it and

its rich posthumous effects. He is always there,
personally with and over it. But in bringing it to
our experience He does not come to it from the
outside, nor simply work alongside. He is immanent always to the Word (for this Word is a
perpetual act); he imbues it, flushes it, brings it,
carries it home from within for the individual soul.
And this not mechanically, by merely making us
acquainted with the Word, and not dynamically,
by the inspiration throbbing in the Word alone,
as if it were driven, like a rocket, with its own
burning; but by a presence and action on each
soul as direct as in the old Word, as intimate
in the sinner as in the Gospel that saves him.
We are raised from our death of sin not simply
by the preaching of Christ's resurrection, but
by the same action of the same Spirit that raised
Christ from the dead. We are regenerate by the
resurrection of Jesus Christ (1 Peter i. 3). The
Gospel is always the Spirit in action, not from
afar, not from an old inspired past which never
loses its force, but also from the direct present
using that timeless past. It is one effect in us
that is achieved vitally by the present Spirit, and
instrumentally by the historic Word. It is the living matter and content of the ageless Word that is
brought livingly home to us by the personality of
the Spirit. Each of the two is necessary to the

one effect of conversion and regeneration. We
must not part the outer and the inner Word, the
past and the present, the Gospel and the Spirit.
This supernature, as Goethe said of Nature, *hat
weder Kern noch Schale*; it has neither husk nor
kernel; all is kernel and all is husk. The Word or
Gospel, like the Spirit, is the holy power of God
acting unto salvation. More than the inspiration
of the Word is required for salvation; the regeneration by the Spirit is required, which seizes and
individualises for us the truest and highest inspiration, renovates it always, and keeps it as near,
fresh, and powerful as life. Even inspiration dies
into the light of common day unless there be a
constant creative power that works it into life's
regeneration.[1] Inspiration visits and impresses
us with fresh light or heat, but the Spirit regenerates us and stays as new life. The power of
conversion is not locked up in the Bible; the Holy
Spirit is always its direct and last cause. But
the Word is His medium; yet 'not as a hammer is
in a hand but as a hand is in the body.' Salvation
is not the effect of genius. We do not do full

---

[1] Again Goethe, with the familiar note that so often drops the
greatest truth in a *causerie* :—

> 'Ardours, like oysters, are excellent food,
> But they must be fresh if they are to be good.
> You cannot bottle inspiration
> Or open, like sardines, on occasion.'

justice to the Bible in magnifying its inspiration
alone. Its unique value is not to kindle but to
create, not to kindle elation but to create life;
not that it is a potent deposit of the Spirit in the
past, but His creative agent always. The virtue
that goes out of the Bible does not get access to
the will (however it impress sensibility) till the same
personal Spirit which acted directly in inspiring the
Bible act directly also through the Bible on the will.

It is useful at this point to stop for a moment
to press the value of this distinction between
impression and regeneration, which for the religious
public is mainly lost. It is a distinction which
becomes very practical in the matter of preaching;
inasmuch as the preaching characteristic of our
day, fine as it may be, is without due power because
it is impressionist rather than regenerative. It is
the servant of religious culture rather than the
source of new life. The connection of this with the
Church's frame of mind in regard to the Holy Ghost
need not be obscure.

If we are acted on only by the content of a
Bible inspired by the Holy Ghost and left to
produce its effect accordingly, one might almost
say naturally, that is but impression. The book
is then the grand classic of religious experience,
extraordinarily effective whether as stirring, impos-

left a beneficent mark on that life. Mysticism, which so readily drifts into a pantheistic religiosity for the lack of a historic anchor, we all own to-day has been of duly priceless service to the depth and beauty of piety when taken in hand. And even a form of spiritualism so wild and bloody as Anabaptism, so solvent of both order and belief, has become, when it was stripped of its ore and moulded in fire, the second great factor of that Independency which has made the modern world. This is a case which the following pages must try to make good.

LECTURE II

WHEN we say, as we usually say, that Independency
was the Reformation coming to its true self, we
may easily fall into a mistake which makes its
history somewhat obscure and leaves much to be
explained. It is not clear, for instance, why Luther's
first instincts that way came to nothing. Certainly
Independency was a true legatee of the Reformation;
and it was so in two directions—in the direction of
personal religion and in the direction of public
freedom, in freedom of soul and freedom of conscience. Especially did it bring to light and to
practice principles which the Reformers themselves
failed to realise in their public effects. Not one of
the leaders surmised, for instance, that in the
predestination which was such a conviction to
them lay the root of modern democracy. Indeed
the fact still seems a paradox to most of ourselves.
They had much to say of a double predestination,
but it was a double predestination in another sense
than theirs—it meant, under the sovereignty of God,

44

not only the foregone salvation of the soul but the
predestined sovereignty of the people. So that,
though Independency did develop the Reformation,
that is only true with two modifications, or rather
expansions. It did most to develop something
else. First, it was not the Lutheran Reformation
it developed but the Calvinistic, not the reformation of prince and peasant, squire and vassal, but
of the free burgher and craftsman, or the yeoman.
It was the civic rather than the agrarian side of
the Reformation it took up on the whole. Yet,
second, it gave distinctive effect to what was but
a collateral of the Reformation, though a factor of
the Reformation age—the radical Co-Reformation,
the persecuted and despised movement of the
peasants and Anabaptists.

How the peasants and the Anabaptists drew
together in Germany is well known. The old
socialist movement of the peasants not only took
advantage of the Reformation to spring to new
life with the reopened Bible, but it joined with a
revival of the old spiritualistic mysticism where
the Spirit took the control from the Word. These
together would have wrecked the Reformation
had the Reformation not wrecked them—truly
under circumstances of barbaric cruelty which
still have their Nemesis in the German Church,
but also under an inevitable necessity, even if

there had been no cruelty beyond what must have
gone with any civil war in such days. Had the
Protestant princes not put down the peasants
Rome would have recovered all she had lost. Not
by such means as crude revolt and Anabaptist
communism could democracy come in; not by the
Spirit without the Word, but only by the Spirit in
the Word, not by Karlstadt or Münzer yet not without them but by Calvin in control of both. But
for Calvin Loyola's counter - reformation would
have recovered all; and the peasant war would
have helped; for it was an uprising of human
nature, and Catholicism, with its Pelagianism, is
the Christianity of human nature. No wonder that
to hierarchical Catholicism Calvin's is a name more
hated than Luther, if less despised. He was the
Loyola of Protestantism, the discoverer of the Reformation future as Loyola secured the future of
Rome, the organiser of its victory for civilisation. He
saved the Gospel, as Loyola has saved the Papacy.

And this Calvin was able to do especially through
one of the two branches into which his movement
spread. For this country these two branches
came into close contact, and finally collision, in
the Presbyterians and the Independents, the
Republicans and the Democrats of their day.
And we may take these names to represent the two
phases of Calvinism to which I allude. It was

Calvinism alone, or that side of the Reformation,
that mostly made the Puritans.   And the unalloyed
outcome of such Puritanism was Presbyterianism.
But Puritanism, on another side of it, came under
other influences.   Calvinism had to be mixed with
another metal to go into circulation as the medium
of the new age.   Through Holland, which became
the refuge of all the remnants of Anabaptism
that were missed by the German sword, spiritualistic and chiliastic influences laid strong hold of
the early Calvinistic Independents, and of many
Puritans who were not yet Independents.   And
these influences worked so mightily that they
ended by capturing Puritanism for that Independency which appealed so strongly to the civil and
local liberty indigenous in the English genius.   For
lack of this kindled public note and popular spirit
Presbyterianism failed in England.   It failed because it was an exotic.   It was too Genevan, too
Scottish, too precisian for the English, and even for
the spiritual, nature.   It was imported and planted
in England, but not acclimatised.   It was 'dumped.'
Like Rome it strove to impose on the English nature
foreign institutions by external force, without
modification, without sympathy, without atmosphere.   Like Rome it was an alien hierarchy, a
theocracy without the free spirit of prophecy, and
without the kind of ideals that appeal to the

heart of a free nation mewing its mighty youth.
Calvinistic popery was no more welcome in England than Roman. Presbyterianism failed, and
left the English future to Independency.

  To say that Independency owed itself to Calvin,
however true, is little more true (if we put it so
baldly) than to say it sprang from Luther. Only in
part does it trace from the canonical Reformation at
all. In great part it sprang from the radical and
revolutionary movement alongside of the Reformation. This was suppressed in the land of its birth,
and in form exterminated, because it had not a
certain secret ; but it was suppressed only to enter
on a risen life, and a more powerful, in England,
where the missing secret was found. The element
always missing abroad was awaiting it here, in the
public, political, and free quality of the English race.
  It is not easy to find a fit name for the whole of
this movement, so tragic, so utterly fruitless on the
Continent. It was so composite of social reds and
spiritual whites, of agitators and mystics, of
tribunes and apostles, of Lilburnes and Foxes. It
has been called spiritualistic, socialistic, and, by
the Germans, enthusiastic. If the word enthusiastic had not received among us a wholly worthy
sense it is the term that would most conveniently
fit the case. And if I use it it will be in the historic

sense. In England the Chiliasts (or Millennarians),
Ranters, Levellers, Anabaptists, Antinomians, Independents, Libertines, Enthusiasts were all names of
parts that were applied to the whole. Apart from
associations Libertines would be a useful term.
Their common feature was the supremacy of the
Spirit to the Word, of the unwritten over the
written Word, of the inner light over outer truth,
of free prophetic individualism over the historical
continuity of the Church. I shall mostly call them
Anabaptists or Spiritualists.

Nothing is easier than to lump the whole im-
broglio of these struggling sects of the seventeenth
century into one contemptible mass, and bundle
it into an abyss of neglect by the sensible man.
But sanity is not the first principle of religion, nor
sound sense the ensign of Christianity. This
treatment is too lordly to be historic, and it betrays
that knowledge without insight which so easily
besets the ordinary capable man—especially if he
study fourteen hours a day.

The source of Independency was Calvinism, its
genius was Anabaptism, its soil was the English
character. Its historical source was Calvinism
through Puritanism; its intrinsic genius was that
enthusiastic Doppelgänger or obverse of the Reformation which we may conveniently call Ana-

D

baptism (though the matter of baptism is quite
secondary compared with the enthusiastic and
spiritualistic note) ; and the soil in which it grew
to its true self was that genius for practical politics,
local self-government, and public freedom, civil
and religious, which is England's note in history.
Independency was Calvinism flushed and fertilised
by Anabaptism on English ground. It drew from
Calvinism its positive and theological Gospel of
the Word, from Anabaptism its personal and subjective religion of the Spirit, and from England
its free constitution of the Church, non-dynastic,
non-territorial, and democratic. Therefore its note is
a founded spiritual liberty, generated from a centre
of Gospel which was theological, and not merely
subjective, in its content, where the spirit did not
override but realise the Word. If we distinguish
spiritualistic liberty as an unchartered religious
subjectivity, rationalistic liberty as an undogmatic
fluidity of belief, and evangelical liberty as the
creative release of the conscience into eternal life
from its guilt and bondage before God, then the
base of Independency is the last, its atmosphere is
the first, and the second belongs to it up to the
point where it begins to imperil the third.

What has been most overlooked by us, in going
back to interpret our genius from our past, is the

motherhood for us of Anabaptism. And among
our sources of satisfaction may be numbered this,
that we rescued this great movement, gave it to
itself, and enabled it to rise purified from its dreadful martyrdom in its native land to become the
most powerful factor in modern history. It is
therefore worth some special attention, in the way
of expanding what I suggested a few moments ago.

The Anabaptist movement, strictly so-called,
was bound up with another, I have said, in the most
fatal way. Anabaptism in itself was a movement of
extreme spiritualism, the crude precursor of all that
has made Quakerism most attractive and effective
to many religious minds of our own day. But where
Quakerism (in connection with Pennsylvania for instance) made friends of the mammon of unrighteous-
ness, and exploited for better things the government
of the time, Anabaptism took the other course, to
its futile doom. It joined itself to the revolutionary socialism of the hour. It was not content to
know that it had, like all Christianity, a political
effect ; it must also adopt a political mission, and
even military methods. And it courted from the
governments the extermination it received. It
committed itself to the peasant insurrection, the
national strike ; and together they made the mystic
socialism, the spiritualistic radicalism, which was
the really popular side of the whole unsettlement

that included the Reformation, and which became
a greater danger to Lutherism for the time than
Rome.   The grievances of the peasants were indeed
intolerable ; but Luther had to tell them that he was
an apostle and not a tribune, that direct redemption
was not the same thing as immediate redress, that
it could not be exploited for prompt social relief,
that the kingdom of God did not come by cataclysm,
and that freedom with God was not at the same
moment freedom from feudal slavery—from rent,
corvée, interest, tithes, and such things as furnished
occasion for the overlord's rapacity and brutality.
They were set for radical reform in economic affairs.
He said that practical religion was experimental,
that the most urgent affair was the soul's with
God, and that reform was not truly radical till it
was regenerative.   Regeneration was the liberty
which the Bible directly promised, and the only
way to the safety and permanence of all social
freedom.   The message seemed to them then, as
to their successors now it often seems, but mockery.
So they stood outside the Reformation as its
popular rival, in the frame of Mr. Keir Hardie's
special hatred for Liberalism ; covering more ground
than the Reformation did, and threatening it more
than it was threatened by the counter-reformation.
Had Luther joined them, probably he and they
would together have been extinguished by the

princes, who were more dynastic than evangelical
still; and with them would have gone all the
Reformation stood for. Europe was not ready in
the sixteenth century for the twentieth—as the
twentieth is not ready even for the twenty-first.
Rome would have been fixed on the West more
firmly than before. The Reformation had positive
realities behind it, the Revolution had but miseries,
despairs, and ideals. And ' spiritualism and idealism are but regulative, they are not creative and
constitutive principles.' They are not the powers
that ride a whirlwind and rule a crisis of the first
rank. It was a dreadful solitude for Luther to
have against him the great Church, the fine humanism, and the maddened socialism of his day, with
all the appeal made by utter misery and true piety
to a humane, to say nothing of a Christian, heart.

The peasant leaders, and especially the Anabaptists, were mostly good Christian people, strict
in life and ardent in soul, full of ethical principles,
impatient ideals, mystical dreams, and social
despairs; they were religious individualists charged
with a literal supernaturalism and denationalised
by long and bitter wrongs. Pacific anarchists by
their nature, the Anabaptists among them have
been called the Tolstoians of their day, opposed to
a state, to war, to punishment, to an organised
and political Church, and to all intolerance. In a

negative form they had many of the conditions of
the religious freedom of the future. They proposed,
quite in Tolstoi's naïve way, to transfer straightway
to the social life of the natural man everywhere the
Sermon on the Mount—which is impossible for the
natural man, and is there only for men waiting on
Christ, men already Christian. They regarded it,
without a vestige of historic sense, as the promulga-
tion of an inspired and imperative constitution for
society. Like all apocalyptics they were innocent
of any historical treatment of the Bible, and they
applied it offhand, with its face value, to the circumstances of the hour. Their failure on the Continent
is another illustration of the fact that, though the
cries, and struggles, and even the principles, of the
oppressed may rouse attention and pose the problem, it is not the oppressed that make liberty
practical politics, but the labour and sacrifice of a
class that stands powerfully between the tyrants
and the victims.

The movement was not called into life by the
Reformation. It was not the radical end of the
Reformation. It did not prolong the Reformation
so much as exploit it. Its ideals were different.
For centuries before such resentments and uprisings
had become as chronic as feudal cruelty. But in
the Reformation this old rebellion found a new
chance. And the popularisation of the Bible gave

a tremendous impulse to it with people for whom as yet every great movement must have religious sanction, who could take the book but in the letter, and who canonised for ever the parousial conditions of the first century of Christianity. This impulse was specially powerful in the Anabaptist circles where the religion was so intimate and personal. There, too, we have a movement which the Reformation did not create. It prolonged medieval mysticism where the peasant rising continued medieval revolt. And it was spiritualistic rather than evangelical. Its note was illumination rather than regeneration, or it was regeneration without the Gospel. Its spiritualism was not made simply by the new accessibility of the Bible ; else we could not account for the totally different effect the Bible had on them and the Reformers, the different ideal of life it gave, and the different object in reform. They were not simply the religious forwards of the Reformation. They were a different movement and an older, which was greatly affected sympathetically by the general disturbance of the Reformation in the whole social and religious system. Both they and the social anarchists harked back not only to prior movements but even to Catholic principles. The roots of Independency lie in a continuity behind the Reformation. The peasants fell back on an agrarian socialism which new economic

conditions had outgrown. And so the Anabaptists
tried to combine a medieval and mystic idea of perfection with a subjective freedom more modern and
more in contact with the Bible. So Anabaptism had
this much in common with the medieval Church—
a one-sided supernaturalism, which it carried to a
head and crisis quite out of tune with the Reformation note. The Reformation broke this abstract,
forced, and hectic spiritualism, which had marked
Catholicism and made the monk. It bred a piety
which worked morally from the conscience outwards.
In Luther monasticism rose ethically from the soul
to the conscience. The Reformation stress was not
on a beatific vision or a rapt ecstasy, but on forgiveness as the regeneration of the conscience.
But spiritualistic mysticism tends to be as unmoral
as it is unhistoric, and it is always impatient of
such a gospel as Luther's, which seems to it to
mark but an early and outgrown stage of the soul.
It speaks so to-day, and it spoke so then. The
Word, it said, is very well, but the Spirit is more and
higher. The Word of salvation is only to set free
a deep spirituality cramped but not sick. It solicits
rather than regenerates. And so the Anabaptists,
and especially one wing of them, fretted under
Luther's gospel of forgiveness as the perpetual obverse of eternal life. They thought the historicism
of the Reformers was the limitation and not the

foundation of Christianity, and that it represented
but a new kind of secularity by comparison with
their own spirituality.   They treated sanctification
too much as the evolution of native spirituality and
too little as the growth of a moral re-creation.   And
from a spirituality merely implanted by the Spirit
of God, apart from the work of Christ, they readily
went on to think only of a spirituality innate but
hampered in the soul of man.   So that in saving
men God rather pressed a button (if one may so
speak) than wiped a slate.   They made too much of
an immediate divine inspiration for each, and too
little of the Bible as the unique and final revelation for all.   For them the Spirit was a new dispensation, and added a new region to revelation.   They
developed the Spirit, not through the Word, but
over its head, and at its cost; and they were the
ancestors of all who find Christ but the chief symbol
of the sacramental agencies which unite the soul
with God.   The Spirit in their personal experience
was coequated with the Bible, of which it really
and practically took the lead.   It was a new and
independent rule of faith (if such impulses had a
rule) rising from deeper depths of man's inner
spirituality under the stimulus of God.   One thing
that drew them to the socialist side was their
proneness to discredit the moral order that
society had already evolved, in order to return to a

putative state of nature prior to the Fall, where
communism prevailed, government was needless,
authority superfluous, and each followed his inner
light, or his immediate divine inspiration. Long
before the Reformation the masses cherished the
mythological idea that personal liberty of a complete and ideal kind was man's first estate, which
had been corrupted and destroyed by tyranny.
Inspiration took the place of faith with these
Spiritualists, as happened also in the case of their
legatees, the Quakers, with a supernatural inner
light, and the Rationalists, with a natural. Their
indifference to the social order was largely due
also to the fact (which had the same effect in New
Testament times) that they lived in constant ex-
pectation of Christ's return in a sudden, speedy,
and purely preternatural way; and they had no
more room or use for the historic evolution of Christian society in the future than in the past. They
were apt also to be held together more externally
by their antipathies than inwardly by their sympathies, which were atomic and anarchic. They
united to resist any historical and organised church,
as their social wing was opposed to the historic
state. The aversion to the Church became centred
and symbolised in their rejection of infant baptism
on its threshold. Their positive bond, in so far as
it was a bond, lay in their appeal to the inner light,

to the individual experience, natural or supernatural, and in their efforts to set up communities of saints and perfectionists, which continually dissolved for want of a thread upon which to crystallise. It will be seen as we go on of what religious value and political importance this last feature became when transplanted to England.

It was only later, only after the bloody death of the whole movement abroad that their gospel of regeneration was regenerated, and its immortal soul rose and entered on its true kingdom here. It produced the Independents and Baptists, who again have been the real founders of modern democracy, in a very modified continuity with the Reformation. It was not peasant wars, nor Anabaptist brotherhoods, nor any mystic or anarchic radicalism that brought in the vast future. It was made by churches and not by groups. Fraternities cannot bring in the great brotherhood. These things by themselves passed like devastating storms—negative and sterile. The peasant rising and the Anabaptist experiments made the German counterpart of the French Revolution. They were equally catastrophic, and in their direct results even more barren. As the fashion of the day was, the movement sought religious sanction and colour. And it thought it found them partially in the work of the Reformers.

Yet the Reformation was not its cause, as I have said. At most it was its opportunity. Still the two streams became so much involved that the Reformers' treatment of the rising did much to discredit and arrest the Reformation, especially on its popular side. It turned the peasantry from it and recatholicised South Germany. The Reformers lost by it, and the princes won. For the medieval theory of the state continued as yet to hold the field. It recovered for Luther himself a hold which had been shaken by the first creative power and logic of his principles. Within a few years he was contradicting as a statesman all he had first said as a prophet.[1] It was not, as Troeltsch says, the Reformation that destroyed medievalism; it was Dissent, it was Independency, and the democracy it made.

The social revolution of that day gathered to the Reformation and tried to exploit it, as its successors have in various forms sought to exploit both a democratic Church, a popular Christianity, and an open Bible. It gathered to the Reformation in a vague response to its note of freedom. But the Reformation was not primarily a battle for freedom. It was much more. It was a battle for the truth

---

[1] See Sippel, *Zeitschrift für Theol. und Kirche*, 1911, Ergänzungsheft iii. p. 104-5.

that makes freedom, for saving truth.   Freedom
was but a means to God's truth and kingdom as
the end.   And it was truth 'activist,' not as knowledge but as reality, as truth of life and action,
as moral effect, as salvation, private and social.
Its question was not social, nor even theological,
but spiritual.   Is salvation direct from God to the
soul, or is it by the mediation of the Church ?   It
declared for the former.   And the whole issue of
freedom was raised by consequence, though sometimes by a long consequence.   For the freedom of
a Christian man did not mean for Luther what came
to be meant by its corollary ' religious liberty,' or
liberty of conscience.   Religious liberty (as I shall
show later) did not mean for him or his a liberty
among men to choose your religion ; nor did liberty
of conscience mean liberty to follow conscience
in spite of society.   It meant something higher
and deeper—freedom before God by God's own
grace in Christ.   It certainly did not mean freedom
to be free from God.   The Reformation freedom
therefore was not the republication of man's
natural freedom revised, but the revelation of a new
freedom only in the Gospel—a freedom by redemption, not creation.   It was therefore freedom of soul,
not either of thought or action.   But it is not
wonderful that another passion, the passion for
social freedom, was the popular passion of the hour.

It is so easy to-day; what must it have been then ?.
The growth of capital, which is given to him that
already hath, and the failure of the ruler's power
to curb the rich, had almost extirpated the free
yeomanry (as has happened under the plutocracy
in our own rural parts). It had gradually reduced
them to vassals, through the mortgage of one after
another of their rights and properties. They were
but tenants of 'led farms' or 'tied houses,' and the
rent which they could not find in cash was taken
to the last farthing in service and dues of various
kinds. The people became serfs in various degrees,
under what was for the most part the worst
brutality. If they had to borrow money it was
from capitalists whose interests were the same as
that of the landowners. The incessant wars added
to these devastations on their holdings. The
bitterness and despair were unspeakable. Anything would be better than what was. Catastrophe
could leave them no worse. The air was full of
imminent convulsion and brooding apocalypse.
Some grand *parousia* might any day arrive and
welcome. The occultists and wizards of all kind
peeped and muttered to the like purpose. This
was the social meteorology of the time. When
the Reformation emerged it diverted attention for
a season. But as evangelical reformation it did
not appeal to the state of mind I have described,

full of wrongs rather than guilt. With misery and despair driving them to hope only in some redress, violent and eschatological, no apostles were likely to be well heard whose whole stress was on the ethical. The voice of reform is silenced in the storm of revolution, and faith seems futile to a state of fury. An ethical gospel can never make direct headway in a time of social convulsion and a falling order of things. The situation repeated in many features that which apostolic Christianity had to face in the first century. Then it was the philanthropy of the first Christians that got a first hearing for their true gospel on any large scale. Unfortunately the course events took at the Reformation was very different; it was associated with extermination rather than benevolence; and the philanthropic development of the new principle, like its missions, did not come for a century or two after it had been at work in other directions. Nor did it arrive in the native land of the Reformation. Indeed two crowning misfortunes befell the Reformation, from which the continent of Europe has never recovered. The first was its association with the territorial princes in the establishment of the Church and in the harrying of the peasants and Anabaptists. That was in Germany. And the second was the Bartholomew in France. The latter was thorough, successful,

and fatal. It destroyed French Puritanism, and
killed the Reformation in France. The former was
not fatal, but it was most disastrous. It destroyed
anything in Germany corresponding to Independency, secluded the country from the best influences
of democracy, and has thrown the cause of progress
and the people too much into the hands of socialism.

Since it was not the peasant war that was transplanted to England, but the other and more
religious element, I may perhaps be pardoned if
I give a little more space to its description. It is
not quite easy.[1] The ban of the Reformers has lain
for long on the great subjective movement of that
time, and caused it to be much neglected and therefore misunderstood. That ban may have been
a historical necessity, like the attitude of the early
Catholic Church to the Gnostics and other heretics of
the day. But in both cases we have become accustomed to take the heretic at the orthodox valuation,
and in many instances the writings in which the
defeated side said what they could for themselves,
have been either lost, deflected, or ignored. We
are either dependent on selections quoted by the
opponents without a context, or we have been
willing to take the orthodox estimate without

[1] The next few pages owe very much to an article on the subject by
Sippell in *die Christliche Welt*, Oct. 1911.

verifying the references by such data as are extant
on the other side.   The existence of Protestantism
in Europe was bound up with the one side, and
naturally that side has monopolised attention, as
Protestantism is still fighting its case.   As a result
we are much in the dark about the precise views
of the non-Catholics outside the Reformation, and
we are apt to think of the whole mass as a tangle
of individual fantasy.   And we lump them indis-
criminately under a variety of names like those
which designate the jungle of sects in our own
Commonwealth time.

But the whole movement is now receiving closer
attention ; and two tendencies within it emerge
in particular, for which it is convenient to select
two names with distinctive meaning, which I have
hitherto used as more or less synonymous.   These
are the *Anabaptists* and the *Spiritualists*, as represented respectively by Karlstadt or Münzer, and
Franck or Weigel.

They were distinguished thus in the main.

In respect of the *Norm*, or standard, the Anabaptists found it in the letter of the Bible, the
Spiritualists in the spiritualising of the Bible, or
in an ' inner word ' quite detached from the Bible.

In respect of *Ethic*, the Anabaptists fell back on
a literal application of the Sermon on the Mount,
as if Christ were the Moses of the new covenant,

E

and came to legislate in that codal sense. They
were therefore firmly set against oaths, war, or
retaliation of any kind—all in a nomistic way.
The Spiritualists also spoke of a new law, but they
meant by it the law written in the heart, and lighted
up by the immediate action of the Spirit. They
were not legalist. The outer act profited little,
the inner frame was all.

As to the *Church*.   For the Anabaptists the true
Church was visible.   It stood on a pact of believers.
Its badge was their baptism on faith.   The Church
was the fellowship of such believers, whose note was
the complete fulfilment of the Christian law—Christian conduct, according to a Christian code.   Purity
was maintained by strict discipline, administered
by the unanimity or majority of the members.
And salvation depended on membership of the
true Church delimited thus.   Infant baptism was
discarded because it was not enforced by Christ,
and because baptism was not a means of grace but
a sign of covenant relationship with God.   The
Spiritualists, on the other hand, held that the true
Church was invisible, and cognisable by no outward signs like sacrament or preaching.   It could
not be constituted by any pact of men, and it had
existed from the foundation of the world.   Its
king was the inner Christ, its law the inner word.
The Lord is Spirit.   It included the devout heathen,

and all who had the Spirit.   It is not necessary to
belong to any visible church, the communion with
Christ and each other is purely inward, and the
membership is known only to God. No human discipline can draw the line. Excommunication is out
of the question, as being dependent on external
standards ; and only the inner spirit can interpret
the outward word. Majorities are always wrong, as
true Christians are always in a minority. Baptism was rejected in either form, or treated only
as an outer form of small value.

It will be seen that while the Independency of
the eighteenth century carried on the Anabaptist
tradition, a considerable section of the Independency of the nineteenth took up the Spiritualist,
and, theologically at least, were more in sympathy
with the Quaker sect.

Both the Anabaptists and the Spiritualists
were exposed to persecution. And both protested
against it. The Anabaptists because they held
that the Christian law of love was intended to
apply to the government as well as to the group.
Both were under the law of nature, and the true
law of nature (the Anabaptists thought, with the
medieval ' sects ') was revealed to be identical
with the Sermon on the Mount. In the great
coming kingdom the Sermon on the Mount would
be the supreme code, both for the State and

the soul.   It was not quite consistent with
this when they thought that once the thousand
years reign of the saints arrived they should
execute the judgment of God on the godless with
the sword.   The protest of the Spiritualists against
persecution was different.   It stood first on the
nature of faith, which was a higher law that the
government ought to respect as a limit on its
power.   Spiritual freedom was spiritually discerned and spiritually legitimated ; and governments should keep within the four corners of their
secular commission.   Besides, they said, external
standards have no relevance to faith.   The letter
of Scripture is at points uncertain, the translation in dispute, the parts are contradictory.   Each
church, too, has its own confession, so none of these
can be the norm of the one Spirit.   Who decides
the true confession ?   Still farther they quoted
Luther himself to prove that false belief was never
suppressed by coercion.   Heresy was a spiritual
thing, and not amenable to the methods of blood
and iron.

As to the *Reformation of the Church* the Anabaptists said the true body of Christ was a visible
community in the apostles' time.   But it had long
vanished, till it was reconstituted by the Anabaptists themselves.   True to their idea of the
Church as invisible, they said the very first church

as visible was not without hypocrites as well as
saints.   Its collapse could only be repaired by a
special divine intervention, attested by such signs
and wonders as the apostles brought.   This had
not yet come, and the Church was still ' in the
wilderness.'   The existing churches had no divine
authority.   True Christians had only one duty—to
prophesy, prophesy, freely, and prepare the way.
But a visible Church was really as needless for
salvation as a written or preached Word.

Some of these considerations are still good and
always true.   But they coexist in an atmosphere
of spiritual Nihilism which was as sterile for practical effect then as we find it to be now.

It will appear that Anabaptism had a certain
church constitution.   It was an organisation of
believers which was democratic in its nature, with
social interests that sympathised much with the
social unrest of the time, tending to communism of a
kind, with much concern for the poor, the sick, and
the orphan, and with offices accordingly—deacons
and deaconesses.   It was poor in ideas and rich
in sympathies (like much beneficent orthodoxy
still), mystic in its piety, and literal in its ethic.
And it had more affinity with Brownist Calvinism
than with Lutheranism. Spiritualism, on the
other hand, had little interest in any constitution
for a church.   It was indifferent or opposed to

official or institutional religion altogether. Spirit
is bound to no forms; all forms can be spiritualised.
It was without the optimism which looks forward
to the thousand years reign, and its tendency was
pessimistic. The world lies in a wickedness which
can only be destroyed. Efforts at amelioration
could only end in disillusioned resignation. Spiritualism was too ideal to be social in its interests.
The ultra-spirituality of its church led to its
practical negation. Its religion became individualist—the alone with the Alone. In so far as it
did become a community it gravitated to Anabaptism, like the Quakers. And its devotion to
the *Logos Spermatikos*, the Christly reason of God
in every man, became detached from mysticism
and readily ran down into rationalism, and finally
into a dialectic chiefly occupied with criticism of
anything like positive religion.

In Independency the influences of Anabaptism
and Spiritualism meet, mix, and often collide. It
represents the mediating position of Schwenkfeldt
rather than either Karlstadt or Franck. And especially so in not recognising any chance assembly
of Christians as a church, but only those equipped
with the apostolic functions of ministers, deacons,
and discipline; and also in refusing to recognise
the Christ in every man as the divine remnant

that had escaped the Fall. This was the chief difference between Anabaptism and Spiritualism. For the Anabaptists, and especially Schwenkfeldt, said that it reduced Christ to be but a partial Saviour, and divided the active power in salvation between man and God. Schwenkfeldt has great value for Independency. Close as he was to the Spiritualists on many points, yet he was nearer to Münzer and to Independency in insisting that the inner Word was the eternal and incarnate Son who entered the man at a certain point of conversion, and made him a new creature. That is the Christ in us. Otherwise, by the presence of the Logos with evil men, we have but a concord of Christ with Belial, and a communion of light with darkness. There could be no talk of each man being a potential Christ, which is alien and even hostile to our belief and our constitution based on it.

But as soon as we recognise the great influence on Independency of this third religious factor in the sixteenth century, beyond Catholicism and the Reformation, as soon as we realise the effect of it acting (through Holland especially) upon Calvinism rather than Lutheranism, we have some explanation of features in Independency which otherwise seem but eccentric. Just as in the Anglican Church, which lingered behind the

Reformation, violent antitheses like Low Church and High seem each able to claim an equal footing in the formularies, because these were in the nature of a compromise, so also with Independency, which was so much beyond the Reformation. The Calvinistic rigour of one age of it, the evangelistic fervour of another, and the mystical or rationalist extravagances of a third, all find some explanation in the composite influences that moulded its plastic time. On the whole, if we leave out for the moment the Calvinism, it was the more positive leading of Anabaptism that Independency chiefly followed. But it was sufficiently affected by the Spiritualistic tendency to account for such fits of theological Nihilism as have recently developed under the influence of rationalist criticism and mystical monism from the nations around. Even when the Monotheism of Israel was well established, the people was not immune from the revival of old pagan tendencies, through contact with the philosophies of the West and the gnosticisms of the East. And Independency, even since it has been set on its positive base for good and all, has had enough sense of a world mission, and it has refused to settle into a mere sect, so far as this—that it has been much coloured, and in corners submerged, by the worldly movements of a critical, social, and philosophic age. To this side we must now attend.

LECTURE III

FROM the point which views Independency as a chief historic factor of the modern political world the Co-Reformation was of more importance than the Reformation. And as this truth has been so much overlooked it is worth some risk of repetition to develop its nature. We have seen its two distinctive elements to be those which are such powerful ferments at this very hour that we think them new—the social and the spiritualistic, with an animus against what is called the theological. Their inner misfortune then was one that recurs now ; they became severed from the evangelical foundation and control of the Reformation Word. And it was the work of Independency in its great age, by restoring that authority, to provide the positive base which alone could bring the other two factors to their own. We should be very clear what these were. The social side I have discussed. We are not done with it yet. What the Levellers showed in the seventeenth century the Christian socialists

73

show to-day. But the other, the spiritualist side, was even more tenacious and influential. The social revolution of the sixteenth century was quenched in torrents of blood. ' No movement ever spent more martyr blood, or to less purpose.' But the spiritualist element survived the massacres as a man who has had the shock and lesson of his life. It was carried by refugees to other lands, and especially to Holland, and thence to England, where it did not so much flourish anew as become transfused with such immense effect into the Calvinism of the Puritan movement as to create Independency. It could not be expected to be on speaking terms with Lutheranism as its persecutor, but it had much to do historically with the Calvinism both of Holland and England. As we have seen, also, there was a gap in the Calvinist doctrine of the Spirit's relation to the Word which gave at least a footing to the spiritualism that tended to detach them altogether. We may therefore, perhaps, not grudge time to ask more closely what was the spiritual meaning of this Anabaptism, as we may agree, generally rather than strictly, to call the enthusiastic religion which tended to look down on the Reformation as but a passage from one slavery to another. And in this lecture I should like to do it from the side which had least theological affinity with the Reformation—from the rationalistic side.

The Reformers broke the Church as the steward of the Spirit and of Grace. In its stead they placed the Bible. But what was the exact connection of the Bible with the Holy Spirit of Grace? What replaces the Church as interpreter of the Bible? Was it the school—the theologians and scholars? Then we have a new hierarchy. For their doctrine was put forth not simply as the science of faith, but as the code which deciphered the Bible, and therefore as the means of salvation. And this doctrinaire hierarchy was in some ways worse than the old sacerdotal. They spoke of the witness of the Spirit; did they mean it? How far did the possession of the Spirit entitle the laity to revise or reject their conclusions?

Troeltsch says four questions arose. 1. How far might personal illumination be detached from the authority of the Bible? How far might the possession of the Spirit—mystic temperament, devout application, or a special inspiration—entitle a man to claim that he had a new contribution beyond what was in the Bible? How far was he the organ of a higher dispensation which did not realise the old but reveal the new, which did not work the old mine but drove a new shaft? How far did the Spirit give new productivity in the present? How far did He give new truth, parallel and coequal with that which He produced in

the first Church ? The Anabaptists answered these
questions on the whole in a Montanist way, by
moving to supersede the Bible in the Spirit's
name, to leave it behind, and to ignore its unique,
permanent, and providential finality in the economy
of salvation. And it will mostly be found (then as
now) that what seemed to be new truths for them
were but reminiscences for the Church—the refur-
bishing of ideas which its genius had from time to
time found in the Gospel but which had not been
organised into the current belief.

2. Where is the real and final seat of revelation ?
Is it in the inner or the outer Word, the experimental or the historic, the unwritten or the written ?
How far is the standard for interpreting the Bible
in the inner light and its seal ?   If the Bible is freely
popularised in respect of its spread must it not be
fully laicised in respect of its meaning ? If it is
put in every one's own hands must it not be read
by every one's own light ? Can it be the layman's
book otherwise ? If it is said that the key is the
Holy Spirit, is not the Holy Spirit the individual-
ising power of God to every man ? If inwardness
and spirituality be the great and final thing where
is there room for any external authority, whether
priest, or theologian, or the Bible itself as a book ?
The supreme meaning—is it not the simple and
obvious one either to each Christian or even to each

man ? It is easy to see the solvent results of such views at a time so theological, when the Spirit's effect was sought so much in illuminationist knowledge instead of moral and social power.

3. How far is the Bible the rule of life ? If we follow its model way of social life, are we not shut up to a radicalism, or a communism, reproducing the conditions of the first century—indifferent to the state, hostile to the world and its culture, other-worldly, sectarian, eschatological, violent, parousial, in its outlook, hoping everything from salvation and nothing from development ? They did not seem to realise that this was making an external authority both of the Bible and of the first century.

4. How far should we repudiate earthly government as due to sin and the mere law of fallen nature ? Does not the principle of the spiritual community destroy a Church of the State, or indeed any community organised on natural lines for spiritual things ? Is Christian ethic merely an expansion of the law of nature ? Is it not a product of special pneumatic revelation to the elect soul ?

The first two of these tendencies continued and increased the various sectarian movements which for centuries had been recalcitrant to Church authority in the name of a mystic spiritualism.

We can see the same thing working in the orders, which, however, the Church had the tact to take up and regularise. Such movements were all fostered by the reaction of religious inwardness from an outward and worldly Church, and by the kind of restlessness that marks a revolutionary time which yet placed a religious hue upon everything.

The two latter tendencies recall us to Wycliffe, and to the various proletarian revolts from the growing abuses to which he gave an utterance so kindled and so keen. The Bible was treated as a republication of the law of nature ; but of nature as it was before the Fall, not since ; for it had since become the mere right of the stronger. Or they fell back on the new nature, as it was in the very first Church, before it was debased by politicians, theologians, and philosophers to the level of the world, with the world's private property, official authority, hard justice, and loveless force. Go back to the Sermon on the Mount, they said, with its reissue of the first ideal state. ' That is God's will for the constitution of society ; and to realise God's will, so clearly put, is our charge.' So far as obedience to that edict of Christ was concerned they thought the reformed parsons were no better than the old priests. Such was the result of treating Christ's words as edicts and His work as a new code.

Then, as now, such views won a very wide vogue, as simple lay-religion or practical mysticism, among the working classes and the small citizens, who found all the theology of grace to be sophistication, and too humiliating for a plain honest man's religion. They were views which became the source and marrow of much in the Anabaptist movements and their associations. There was an almost angry impatience of the evangelical movement of the Reformation; and not because it was theological (for that was no fault in those days) but as it centred in the forgiveness of sin. Redress and reform filled the hour. There was a vehement reaction against such theology, against any theological theocracy, as also against the association of Christianity with Church order, social position, or political authority. But the aversion was not to theology as such. Some instructed and gifted theologians helped the movement, like Franck and Weigel, whose views it is more than interesting to summarise at a time like the present. They show the antiquity of modernism, as a similar study of Gnosticism would show it in the second century.

Sebastian Franck was a modernist with a wonderful vivacity of mind and gift of style, whose theology was briefly this. He was quite indifferent to historic Christianity, and that in the name of the

Christian spirit. The truth and power of God was inborn in man, and inalienable. It had indeed become obscured by sin, so that it came to its own only through a struggle between the Spirit and the flesh. But for the victory no external or historic aid was required. The historic Jesus dissolved into the eternal Christ logos in humanity, some vital and potent fragment of which was in every man, and was equal to his restoration if he would. The only value of the gospel history was symbolic, suggestive, and evoking. It made us aware of our subliminal resources, of our innate Christ, of a holy spirit of our own.

Weigel is still more explicit and systematic. He is modern enough to be even psychological. What man receives from without is not revelation, not knowledge, and not even impression, but only stimulus. The external history is a mere touch on a button, as it were, which releases the native power of the human spirit into consciousness of itself. It is a mere solicitation or provocation of the excellent soul. It puts into action the wondrous spiritual machinery of man. The Word, therefore, spoken or written, can but awake a man to his inborn and inalienable spiritual resources, and make him aware of the God always immanent in him and in due time becoming conscious. Personality is independent of history, and therefore of Jesus Christ, except as a mere means of edification, a mere symbol of a principle, and a mere expression of the Christ immanent in the constitution of humanity. The Bible has to make itself good before this inner Christ and native forum of the Spirit. It is to be accepted only in so far as it agrees with the eternal Word of God written in human nature at its best. It is not a means of grace, certainly not a unique means, nor is it any exceptional revelation.[1]

But Franck and Weigel represent only one side of the Anabaptist movements—the rationalist and naturalistic side with which the extremists have made us familiar to-day. There was a second group, as I have already indicated, which also postponed the Word, but which made much more of the evangelical base, the real regeneration, and the supernatural Spirit. They were represented by Karlstadt, Münzer, and especially Schwenkfeldt; and it was they whose tradition, through the Dutch Mennonites, acted most strongly on Independency, and also generated Quakerism. It might almost be said that Schwenkfeldt was the first Independent. They believed in a distinct and direct action of the Holy Spirit on the human, coming *ab extra*, and at particular moments. Some of them thought of it as the source of new illuminations, others as the

[1] Franck's date is 1499-1542, and Weigel's 1533-88.

F

source of new power, according as their interest was in truth or in life. The former, like the apocalyptics and visionaries both of the early Church and of our own, gave great weight to the historical revelation in Christ, but they urged that it did not end revelation. They worthily desired to realise God as the constant light and close guide of every man at every hour ; but what they called fresh revelations were really no more than the flashes which the new juncture or the new thought struck from the old Word. They made much of that Word, if not all. What was wrong was their theology rather than their practice. Schwenkfeldt was very urgent about the immediate action of the Spirit of God in a religious and moral re-creation, which the naturalistic wing would have thought uncalled for, or would have treated as a mere waking of us up to our native resources. But he confined the function of the Word to the mind only. It informed us of truth. But it could give it no access to our inner man. The truth of the Word was still an external and noetic thing. The Word is a mere sign, an alphabet, a written symbol. It was not sacramental. It did not, could not, convey itself to the soul. Schwenkfeldt was the victim of a false theory of knowledge, in thinking that there was nothing sacramental in what came by eye or ear, that it was not charged with spiritual signifi-

cance. The knowledge given by the Word was
spiritually useless, he thought, till it was taken up
and turned to account by an action of the Spirit
quite subsequent and independent of it (and then
only for the predestinate). This inner action of
God on the elect was independent of the historical
work of Christ. The outer Word received its
spiritual content only from the spirit-filled man.
Schwenkfeldt reproduced in respect of history Cole-
ridge's subjective fallacy in respect of Nature—

> ' O lady, we receive but what we give,
> And in our life alone does Nature live.'

His religious relation to the historic Christ was
much closer than his theological—which was very
well for him, but ill for those he taught, and,
especially, for those he influenced so widely apart
from personal contact. Personal sanctity may
carry off lack of culture, and pastoral efficiency may
more than make good theological deficiency, but
not for the great public, and not for the next
generation. Piety is the religion of the individual,
but theology is the religion of the generations.
And Schwenkfeldt forgot, besides, that we know
of Christ only through the Bible and the Church,
that a saving Christ could only be transmitted
by a sacramental testimony and not merely an
informational, and that therefore Word and Spirit

were not merely in contact but in organic unity and
reciprocity from the first. But like many devotees
both of his own time and ours, by a mystic immersion in spirituality, he formed a speculative
idea how God should act, and then construed the
past accordingly, instead of reading God's actual
will out of His historic revelation. But there is
more excuse for us than for him ; for he did not
face a history which criticism had made for so many
a tremulous haze.

It will be clear that Anabaptism was not a
movement like orthodox pietism. We are often
accustomed to associate a vehement spirituality
with a somewhat stiff and conventional creed. But
that is partly a result of the pietistic movement,
which came much later, and the evangelical movement which was later still. These wore an animated
orthodoxy which Anabaptism did not. It is partly
due also to the suggestions which the name contains
of continuity with the Baptists and their views.
The Anabaptists were everything but orthodox. At
the same time (as I have shown) they were not all
rationalists in the sense that that word has borne
since the illuminationism of the eighteenth century.
They were heretical saints rather than heretical
philosophers, and, apart from their opinions, are
better represented by Karlstadt and Münzer with

their direct supernatural illumination by the Holy
Spirit, than by either Franck or Weigel with their
natural light from the human spirit. No doubt the
movement tended in its grandchildren to a bald
rationalism, but it was not Socinian in its first
note, though Socinianism, like other things, found a
ready soil in it. It represented, as a whole, mantic
heresy rather than rationalist, prophetic error rather
than prosaic, the heresy of the self-taught preacher
rather than of the too-schooled thinker, of gracious
unction rather than lucid insight, of confident
intuition rather than sceptical thought. Its atmosphere was religious rather than rational or even
idealist—though our later idealism is its adult
stage, when philosophy takes the place of theology.
Some of these pneumatics (as I say) relied on
the inner light as a native spirituality in man,
some trusted in it rather as a supernatural visita-
tion. But both sections severed the Spirit from
historic revelation, and declared that the region of
revelation was extended in matter, and not simply
deepened in appreciation, by the new dispensation.
They did believe in the Spirit, especially against the
world; and there was an intimacy, purity, and passion in their religion not always guaranteed by a
truer faith. But the Spirit took the place of the
Word, and ultimately a higher place. Its voice
was in the ecstatic experience, the conscience, or

the reason. And the constant gravitation of the movement, in proportion as it sought to be intelligent, was to a rationalism whose light became very dry as the first glow of the elation faded; which is the natural history of the doctrine of the inner light everywhere as the rule of faith.

To sum up therefore, the whole tendency may be described as a mystic radicalism, a romantic socialism, a spiritualistic lay-religion which makes little of Christ's priestly work or final word, being preoccupied very excusably with present ills, present impulses, and visionary hopes, but devoid of historic sense, historic continuity, practical policy, or any grasp of the unique place of the Bible, the Church, or the Saviour, in the economy of providence or the making of the soul. It drew largely on the *Theologia Germanica*, as our modern altruistic positivism (in George Eliot for instance) used the *Imitatio*. Its notes are gathered up as the enthusiasm of the inner light, the detachment of the religious community from the state and the world (which meant much more than separation in our sense), the sanctity of brotherly love and spiritual comradeship, quietist submission to persecution, and the conversion (and therefore the debasement) of Christianity from a new creation to a new law, chiefly codified in the Sermon on the Mount. Generally

it substituted the Gospels for the Gospel; it
appealed from an organised church to a mystic
fellowship of the pious democrats and the oppressed;
and it took social form in a loose congeries of groups,
spiritual and futurist, whose function was mutual
comfort and edification, with no church preaching
a commanding gospel to the world. They had many
gifted and even original leaders, who were often,
however, more interesting than fertile, more illumin-
ative than regenerative, more genial than apostolic,
preachers rather than theologians, and preachers
of goodness rather than grace, hierophants whose
theology was hierophantastic, and whose truth
came as rain on the mown grass, or as gleams
through the clouds, rather than as the solar power
from a centre that continually renovates, animates,
and orders all. Their aim, in so far as it was theological at all, was a simple lay Bible theology, without
either science or imagination. They were unversed
in the moral psychology either of holiness or sin;
and they repudiated, therefore, what they called the
artificial theology of the great reformers, who really
reformed, where the spiritualists only renounced,
the great penitential tradition of the Church of
Redemption. Many of them (as I have said), following the spiritualistic line, developed the inner light
as the most pious Quakers subsequently did who inherited their strain. But many also developed it

later on other lines. They denied the Godhead of
Christ. They separated the ideal or spiritual Christ
from the historic. They cultivated an undogmatic
religion, a spiritual agnosticism, with an unlimited
tolerance which meant no positive gospel, but only
a mystic and ethical religiosity. They spiritualised
heaven and hell, and in their philosophy were
monistic, or panentheistic at best. And they
show what our own day shows, that, as soon
as the hold of the historic gospel is lost, the
natural man asserts itself from age to age in quite
a monotonous and venerable way by a natural
theology more or less spiritualised.

It will have been clear that their objection to the
Reformers was twofold. They resisted the State
Churchism which so early took possession of the
Reformation; and here they were prophetic, but
more prophetic than effective. And they took
exception to the great Reformation principle of
faith in grace, which reconstructs everything
from one new creative centre of forgiveness and
redemption. They objected to the Reformers'
interpretation of grace as mercy. If the Romanists
represented one extreme, in which grace was a
sacramental and infusory thing, the Anabaptists
represented the other, so familiar to us, wherein
grace is the general favour and fatherliness of God,
whose benedictions were always dropping silently

into the bosom of His children.   Grace meant any benediction from God's kindness, whether it released the conscience or only blessed it, whether it produced a new creation or only a new refreshment. The grace which had mercy on our guilt was not the central or recreative thing, but only one of the modes in which God's general and unfailing kindness acted according to need.   In Luther's sense of the word it was not needed by all, nor by all who did need it was it needed equally.

Troeltsch, who has interpreted this side of the Reformation age with extraordinary insight, finds such aspects of it very congenial.   He is especially drawn to Sebastian Franck (who is indeed attractive enough), and he roundly declares that modern Protestantism is nearer to Franck than to Luther. That is a judgment of tremendous significance. It is as if it were said that an enlightened Phariseeism was a truer legatee of Christ than Paul was. It means that evangelical Protestantism has simply a historic value, which every year that passes makes more archæological.   The whole movement of theological liberalism and modernism, Protestant or Roman, seems agreed to evict Reformation Christianity in so far as it is founded on an evangelical crisis of the soul, and to take rational possession of its assets in the name of a highly spiritualised naturalism.   The rational and illuminationist reformation overleaps, with some contempt, the reformation of moral re-creation, which by the aid of modern psychology it endeavours to explain away. In his analysis of historic causes and movements, however, Troeltsch is admirable and original, and, except Weingarten, no German has done such justice to English Dissent.

LECTURE IV

THE Anabaptists (it may have appeared) in one way went back behind the Reformation, and in another they went forward far beyond it. Ethically, evangelically, they were in reaction, religiously they were in advance. They left the world to go unto the Father, but they also left the Word to go to the Spirit; and leaving the Word they left the Son, and therefore the Father's final will.

1. They went behind the Reformation in attaching themselves to the medieval note of mysticism, non-historic, and non-moral, and in going round the most new and positive moral factor in the Reformation. The Reformation, like English Nonconformity, restored the moral passion of the Christian idea in the New Testament, its rugged, invasive, miraculous note, its radically new creation, which medievalism, under classic and urbane influences, had erased. It made the soul's religious relation with God a moral thing in a way not only radical but revolutionary, by healing a breach which meant to the conscience not simply damage but dam-

nation. It made religion a thing of God's righteousness, and therefore made it the life indeed. It made
the true inwardness a matter, not of intuition, or
sensibility, or temperament, or any such pious
thing but of a world-forgiveness, regeneration, and
eternal life. It was a theology of fact more than of
consciousness. It thus raised its evangelical protest
against mere moralism in the region of the conscience, and against mere elation or pantheistic fusion
in the region of the soul's communion with God.
To the Anabaptists all this seemed forced, elaborate,
unlaical, and even ethically dangerous. Their lay-
religion was not universal priesthood but simple sonship. They pressed beyond a reckoned righteousness in faith to an actual righteousness in conduct
and experience ; and they did so in a plausible way
which is still very familiar and seems very businesslike, simple, and common-sense. The question only
begins to be acute when we press on to ask—experience of what ?   And as it grows acuter the answer
grows pointed and thorough, it grows theological.
There is no doubt that if it be lay-religion to discard
theology it must be lay-religion also to go on and
discard historical Christianity, as the Anabaptists
tended to do. For historical Christianity, the
Christianity of the New Testament, is theological.
It is not simply spiritual. It is not simply pious.
It is not simply genial. It is not simply filial.

So far as this goes Anabaptism was reactionary.
It was but Judaism spiritualised by contact with
Greek idealism, Judaism neo-platonised. And it
showed it in its ethic, which was ascetic, meticu-
lous, synagogual, conventiclist, what would now be
called seminarist, and savoured of the Nonconformist conscience in the inferior sense of that ambigu-
ous term. Whereas the good side of the State
Churchism of the Reformation, continued in
Cromwellian Independency, was that it had a
more actual historic influence and a wider historic
outlook. Its ethical principles, as they were
practical and corporate, so were national; as they
were radical, so were universal; as they sprang
from the soul new created to its last base, so also
they were on the scale of the whole world. It is a
curious thing, but it is possible for a movement or
a church to be very evangelical on the extensive
scale but not evangelical at all on the intensive.
That is to say it is Low Church. It spreads its
gospel over the face of the earth, but not into the
thought and temper of the age. It covers, but it
does not leaven. It does not recreate the age's
habit of mind, or affect at all its culture, while it is
tremendously earnest and enterprising in gathering
converts in from the whole world. That is why
missions, which owe so much to Low Church, are
losing their staying power. They spread the Word

rapidly—but so thin that it cracks. The Reformation, on the other hand, aimed at mastering civilisation and not merely protesting and withdrawing from it. It aimed at mastering civilisation rather than covering the world in missions. It would make civilisation itself first Christian and then missionary; and so it would abolish the chief drawback which missions experience in the paganism of the civilisation from which they go. And though it has too often been victimised by the civilisation it sought to convert, such conversion of affairs was at least its aim. It contemplated a Christian world, and not a sectarian, or a chiliastic. The *lex naturae* to which it went back was what it actually found, as the medieval legacy of a church not wholly deserted by the Spirit of God; and it set to work on this concrete situation and modified it by its new idea of faith. It did not call society a *massa perditionis*, nor government a mere consequence of the Fall. It left the natural constitution of man and his *justitia civilis*, his civic righteousness, undestroyed by the Fall, however damaged. It did not believe in total corruption, but only in total helplessness to regain communion with God.

With the Anabaptists it was otherwise. They reverted, in a monastic way, to some imagined, perfect, and prehistoric state. They lived therefore in a world of isolation, elation, and catastrophic hopes. Like most radicals, and all revolutionaries, they had no historic sense. They simply resumed the anti-secular note of the first century, with its sharp parousial supernaturalism; and they cultivated a literal Biblicism, in spite of the fact that they repudiated the external authority of Church, Bible, and dogma. Even within the Bible they preferred the Sermon on the Mount to St. Paul, like Erasmus, from whose pupils they got much help.

They represent in truth the second great movement of a long, old tendency, whose first movement filled the early centuries, and whose third fills the present day—that constant tendency, which I discussed at the outset, to detach the Spirit from the Word, to naturalise faith, and so to idealise Christianity as to de-historicise it. The vice of this detachment of the Spirit from the Word is that it ends by destroying its detachment from the world. Detached from the Word, the supernatural action of the Holy Spirit becomes gradually the natural evolution of the human spirit. The Spirit becomes identified with the natural humanity. A real distinction between the Spirit and the world ceases to exist, in the absence of the evangelical crisis of the Word. This detachment from the Word we have seen to be an old tendency of the

spiritual life. The Gnosticism of the second
century, the Spiritualism of the sixteenth, and the
Protestant liberalism or Roman modernism of the
twentieth all represent outcrops of the same pagan
tendency to replace faith by insight, to make mere
inspiration do the work of revelation; they idolise
the immediate preaching and despise the objective
theology (which alone provides the preacher with
a gospel outside his subjectivity); they think much
of the man who makes religion a treat and little
of the man who makes it real and true; they gather
about those who exploit God as man's great asset
and neglect those who would subdue man as God's
great instrument; they listen to men who urge faith
with no power to produce it, and ignore those who
are engrossed with a worthy and positive object of
faith which alone can create it. The Reformers
lived with the note of revelation, on a theology of
facts; the Anabaptists with the note of inspiration,
on a theology of consciousness. The one set were
apostles, the other prophets. For the one the Spirit
issued from the Word of gospel, for the other it
wandered like the wind and was its own gospel.
We shall see that, as the vice of the one was to
dry into a hard orthodoxy severed from experience,
the vice of the other was to deliquesce into a vagrant
experience on whose bogs flitted the enticing fire-
drakes of subjective whim. Each is invaluable in

its own place and power. The gospel must be a kindling and present experience; but a kindling and present experience is not necessarily the gospel. It was Independency that really welded them, united and fertilised them, proclaiming a pointed and positive gospel, with a wide range for thought and comprehension in a vivid personal experience. The Christian gospel escaped from Calvinism, from the systematic creed of the Puritans, by the aid of ardent Anabaptism; but only to return for protection from its Anabaptism to the cardinal Calvinism in which it first rose. Anabaptist freedom, which has been such an invaluable servant, would have been a fatal master. But the return in men like Cromwell or Goodwin was to a Calvinism more precious for its positive evangelical centre than for its dogmatic symmetry, for its creative foundation than its closed system. Independency returned, on its native Calvinistic lines but with great new liberty, to the common faith of the Reformation; where it must always stand, or else go to dust as the mere sanctuary of every error and the consecration of every whim.

In the history of Independency itself we may mark in small the same tendencies and the same movements as we have just noted in the Church at large—the tendency especially to a creedless

subjectivity—to stray in the Spirit too far from
a positive base in the Word for unity or effective-
ness, to lose touch with the apostolic Word and
Reformation gospel, and to covet another liberty,
with another Lord, who is no Lord but only
hero, prophet, master, or ideal. And we shall see
that the great problem of the present moment for
Independency is not how to extend its action but
how to re-assert its base. It is not to parade liberty,
which grows thin as it grows thrasonic, but to regain that firm height and revisit that living spring
whence freedom flows as sweet as mountain streams,
and as irresistible as the river they make.

The influence of Anabaptism tended to carry
Independency round the outside of the Reformation
and give it a medieval and Catholic connection
which did not exist for either Presbyterians or
Methodists. And, strange as it may seem, this is
one of the sources of our intellectual liberty, and
our affinities with Roman modernism. That
modernism is not simply a reaction and a rebound
from medieval theology ; it is to a large extent a
development of it, of its temper and method if
not of its positions. It develops those mystic and
intellectualist sides which the Reformation passed
by. It passed by them and their notion of freedom
to seize on the ethical and evangelical release which

made the true apostolicity of the Church, and which was preserved, in spite of the schoolmen, by the priest's practical contact with sin in the great penitential tradition of the Church. As often as I spoke with the late Father Tyrrell I felt that his immersion and mastery in medieval scholasticism had much to do directly with the modernism which grew upon his Jesuit days, and with his lack of sympathy for the sharp evangelical issue of the Reformers (which was due also to the debased evangelicalism that surrounded his early days). For modernism is a latter-day scholasticism, where Hegel, or some other recent philosopher, takes the normative place of Aristotle. It is intellectualism, either mystic or æsthetic in tone, and socialised by the interests of a Church or of the State. And if more people within the Congregational than, say, the Presbyterian, pale are found to be in tune with this anti-evangelical modernism, with the theological side of liberal intellectualism rather than with a liberal but positive theology, then some part of the explanation may be found in the direction I point. Leaving inferior causes on one side, it is partly due to the Anabaptist (*i.e.* medieval) tradition in Independency, which gives it an extra-Reformation strain, and a bias to mystic rationalism. But it is this same cause also which has happily pro-

tected it from the sympathies shown by other
bodies for an ultra-evangelism; and especially
from those imported evangelistic movements which
are associated with a narrow Biblicism, a hard
asceticism, and a type of religion with a snap
action and a metallic note.

Of all the free churches Independency is least
directly due to the Reformation, least bound by it,
and therefore most free for it.

2. But in Anabaptism there was not only the
tendency to go round the Reformation, and seek
outside its evangelical liberty the inner freedom
and mystic haven of those oppressed under the
medieval Church. There was another principle at
work, and a greater, of which it was but partly
conscious, as of our true greatness we mostly are.
It did something else than pick up with an ineffectual past; it cherished under its heart a
mighty future. If it wedded the one it bore
the other. It was the prophet, not to say the
agent, of a world-future. Its inward and passionate personal religion carried consequences, once it
was married to the Reformation gospel, which produced the English revolution of the modern world.
So long as the inwardness was all and the form
nothing, Anabaptism was ineffective, except to
produce the religious subjectivity, the ineffective

spiritualist egoism and sentimentalism which is
not unknown in later revivals. But when that
earnest inwardness was saved from its own inner
weakness by union with the English genius leavened
by free grace, it became the mother of public
liberty in the modern world. It is true that the
rights it first claimed were supposed to belong
only to the regenerate, and not to the universal
man, to the sect and not to society. And its
freedom of belief was the Spirit's working within
its own pale, it was not the mere rational liberty
of the natural man. It was the freedom of the
reborn not the freeborn. But such rights and such
freedom had too much of the instinct of a universal
gospel to stop at these narrow bounds. And
through Independency they passed to create the
best phase of modern liberalism. The spirit of
its high calling was not tractable to the powers
or principles of the old order of things. ' To every
single religious community the right belonged
to the free and sole disposal of its affairs. And
this autonomy became the foundation of the
doctrine of the sovereignty of the people, which
in practical form it introduced into the world.'

Liberalism never became a danger, either as
theological or political, so long as it grew in the
congenial soil of a positive gospel, so long as the
free Spirit flowed straight from the emancipating

Word. The Reformers had this creative and regulative Word, the Anabaptists had the inspiring and kindling Spirit. The problem was to reconcile them. And it was so substantially and thoroughly done in Independency that its Church principle was carried into modern affairs. But it was not done by the direct identification of the Spirit with the reason, or the inner light with the Logos in human nature. That way lay Deism and all its train. To call in the laws of natural reason or utility to control an inner light which was the experience of a new life in the Holy Spirit—it were as if St. Paul had invited ephors or lictors to regulate the charismatic disorders in his Corinthian Church. Nothing but the Word of the Gospel has the right to order the Spirit of the Gospel, an evangelical faith to control a pneumatic.

Three things should be clearly realised. First, what I have already urged, the extent to which Independency was not only affected but made by Anabaptist influences, entering especially through Holland, and culminating in Cromwell's army. Anabaptism and Independency had in common such ideas as the Church's freedom from the State, congregational autonomy, the democratic constitution of the Church, purity of communion confined only to the regenerate, repudiation of a

liturgy to give free play to the Spirit, reduction of
the sacraments to symbols or pledges, and to a
large extent Calvinistic dogma. The Independents
represented the individualism both produced and
quelled by predestination, in a combination with
Anabaptist inwardness, and English self-government. When this combination took hold of the
Commonwealth army the modern world was born.

Second, we should note the way in which, when
these Anabaptist influences had done their work,
they were rejected by Cromwell and the great
Independents. By closing down, with an Anabaptist intimacy of experience not only spiritual
but evangelical, on the central Reformation gospel
as the touchstone of Christianity, they shed the
zealots; and they at once saved historic Christianity from being lost, and Independency from
sharing the fate of continental Anabaptism. ' In
Cromwell Anabaptism reaches its summit; but
all the same it was by Cromwell's act that
Anabaptism by itself ceased to be a historical
power.' He was for liberty to all Christians; but
these were defined neither as creedalists nor as
spiritualists, neither as legalists nor as libertines,
but as people who lived the saved life of faith in
the atoning Son of God. He and his great theological advisers reacted from pure spiritualism,
but it was into evangelicalism, and not into con-

fessionalism ; it was into the Reformation Word
of a central forgiveness and redemption as the
power creative of the Christian society. On this
base they aimed (too credulously at first) at a
democratic franchise both in Church and State,
a vital and enthusiastic inner religion, and a strict
ethic. There was great freedom of conscience
but none in morals, and there was room to think
freely but not to live laxly. There was no effort
at uniformity of doctrine. They believed for
freedom's sake in firm declarations (like the Savoy)
of what real Christians did believe, but not in
creeds of what they must believe. They had little
interest in school theology ; their treatises were
sermons. Their theology was not metaphysical ;
it was organised experience, systems of profound
religious psychology. It was, so far as that experience went, a lay-religion ; but it was the
religion of laymen of living faith, who had passed
from death to life by Christ's cross, who lived
that life upon their Bible, and interpreted it in
the Holy Ghost by sanctified common-sense applied
to individual experience of the evangelical kind.
All theology was relative and free inside that
revelation in Christ which was creative of their
spiritual life.

Under the rule of the ' saints ' all views and
denominations had been free within the pale of

Christ's grace, and they insisted on moral uniformity only. Rigid theology and easy livers were both banned. Dogma was free, polity was free, only ethic was fixed in relation to the world, and, within the Church, the life of grace. But the obverse of that generous liberty was, at this stage, and in the masses of the people, something like chaos. Extravagance and fanaticism abounded. Subjective liberty came to be prized more than the gospel charter of it. Eccentricity, confusion, and even anarchy had full scope. The Levellers would level all belief as well as all status to equal value. Inspiration was personal suggestion or passing fancy. And the Bible, once the product of inspiration, now became its prey. The charismatic conditions of the time corresponded to the state of things in which each neophyte or amateur is a law to himself, with a passion and claim to urge on others whatever strikes him, and to urge it as God's latest will.

These were circumstances which made absolutely necessary some clear and positive return to a ruling and organising centre both for life and doctrine, even if it came by a dictatorship. And Cromwell was on the spot with his evangelical positivity as well as his political mastery. Neither his religion, his culture, nor his statesmanship could tolerate the zealotry and anarchy which were dissolving faith, pulverising society, threatening the univer-

sities and thereby the pulpits, and reducing the
Church to a mere frantic fraternity. Could he
only have done it by other than military means !
We face like dangers not only without but within ourselves. But we have learned to use other
means—when we are sufficiently alive to the danger
to be roused to use means at all.

And, third, we must keep in view the transfer
to politics of the Church principles of Independency, and especially that of the sovereignty of the
democratic people, or the conversion of Independency into political liberalism. The nature of this
process is well explained by Bougeaud in his *Rise
of Modern Democracy*. It was a step fraught with
enormous consequences to both Church and State
—for the public a great blessing, and nothing less
also to the Church, so long as it remained more sure
of its bondage to Christ than of its freedom among
men. When the sense of that relation to Christ fails,
through a gospel diluted or displaced, where truth
is lost in freedom, not only does the democracy
lie open to its serious critics, from Aristotle to
Montesquieu, but its moral sanative, the Church,
becomes much more politicised by the State than
the State becomes Christianised by the Church.
To a large extent these inferior influences resurged
upon the Commonwealth Independency through
the army, and through the fact that it conquered

by an army. No doubt an army is effective.
Anybody can govern with grape-shot for a time.
And then———. Let us beware of the idolatry of
efficiency. It is as dangerous as the cult of incompetence. It ends in the spirit of militarism.
Let us care more for a man's competency than for
the efficiency of a scheme. Competent men will
in the end do slow justice to a principle which a
swift efficiency may wound to kill.

It is quite true that the State was looked down
on by the Anabaptists. Natural justice and
civil order were not yet for them invested with
a right equally real with that of the religious
community (however different), and equally (though
differently) based on the conscience. Yet by their
share in Independency they made this larger and
more historic view possible. It certainly did not
grow out of Reformation State Churchism. It
grew from the union of Anabaptism with radical
Puritanism. Puritanism corrected Anabaptist extravagances, both social and theological, while
itself became much tempered by Anabaptist
inwardness and liberty. It was the firm but
liberal dogmatic base laid by the Calvinistic
side of Independency that saved for the future
the precious elements that were running to waste
in Anabaptism, the absorbing personal piety, the

warmth of immediate experience, the germs of modern, critical, and historical freedom, the notion of universal religion, and especially its political, social, and ecclesiastical effects. And the moral is still—beware of mere churchless, creedless enthusiasm, whether the enthusiasm of humanity or of spirituality. Beware of a mere democratic spiritualism, a popular spiritualistic pantheism, or even a simple Fatherhood, detached from a positive saving Word.

It may readily be asked here how Independency justified itself in transferring directly to civic society the social principles which ruled its Church life, and in making its high spiritual polity the law of the natural society. Were there not conditions and powers peculiar to a Christian society like the Church, which alone could ensure the due control and safe working of democratic principles ? Was the Church not founded in an obedience of which natural democracy knows nothing, but which yet is freedom's moral salvation ?

To that question the answers are several. We must return to the subject, but some may be given here.

In the first place, there were in those days none who did not belong to some Church, and therefore none who were quite disentitled to Christian liberty. The nation was the Church. The time had not yet come when the nation contained a vast de-churched mass in all classes. That on the one hand.

And, on the other, Independency, here as else-where, did not simply take Anabaptist sectarianism and swallow it whole. It did not regard all state authority and civic life as a consequence of the Fall, and strive, by ignoring civil history and society, to return to conditions purely supralapsarian. It did not seclude itself, as the continental sects did, from its social world. It did not say there was nothing in common between the civic order and the spiritual group. It did not cherish the theology of total corruption. It had a divine *justitia civilis* amid the wreck of spiritual righteousness. Human nature and its laws were not pulverised by the Fall. Its constitution was not dissolved. The *lex naturae* was still the law of God as far as it went. Independency here followed the Reformers, who exempted from the effects of the Fall the whole region of social order. They held that what was broken was not civic righteousness but the soul's relation with God ; and what was destroyed was not human nature's divine constitution, but its will and its power to set itself right with God. It retained civic order and virtue. What it had not was the power of self-salvation and of society's final and godly consumma-

tion. So that it was not a case of transferring to the
public in a lump the freedom of a closed aristocratic
sect, like the pure Anabaptists, but of recognising
a common civil freedom as God's inalienable gift.
Neither was it a case of transferring to the public
the whole powers and liberties of the Church.
The sovereignty of the people was their autonomy
in these civil and secular affairs, and not in all.
It was arrested at the threshold of the Church.
It did not enter the region of the saved conscience,
where Christ alone was King. The sovereign people
could impose no obligation coming between the
Church's conscience and its loyalty to its Saviour.
So that we have the sovereignty of the people in
worldly affairs, and of Christ in spiritual. And the
same Christian principle as made the democracy
also secluded the Church from its control as the
reserve of Christ, and made it a free Church.

And, to recall the more practical and political
considerations prescribed by the historical situation, it was impossible at that juncture to assert
spiritual liberty without civic because of the Stuarts'
fatal identification of the cause of Christianity with
episcopacy, and episcopacy with monarchy. The
protest therefore for a free worship and a free
Church became necessarily a protest against royal
prerogative in the name of the ruling people.

LECTURE V

To arrive at the true genius of Independency we need concern ourselves less with its early stages of Brownism, Penryism, Barrowism, etc., than with its brief blossom and creative revelation in the Commonwealth. For it is not like the Reformation movement, or the Wesleyan, or even like Christianity itself, which had their origin in one commanding and creative personality. Its earliest exponents were but harbingers of what should come rather than apostles of what had come. For instance, much early Independency was not democratic, or at least not clearly so. It was but feeling its way to democracy; and it was not clarified in this respect till after its conflict with the aristocratic Reformation in Presbyterianism. It was in the brief Commonwealth that it arrived at its true consciousness of itself, and realised its true idea. Unfortunately, while the idea was quick and powerful, the form which circumstances forced on its expression was too alien at heart to its genius to be permanent. It was too forcible, sweeping, and

111

military. Its mood was too imperative for the minority it was. Cromwell therefore died and failed (some would say failed and died). But his spirit nevertheless passed into Independency for good and all; as Caesar, in spite of his death, or by it, made the Roman Empire, made it a Caesarism and, in its supreme Church phase, a Caesaropapism. Cromwell, a more sacred Caesar, is the Independents' man of men; meaning by Cromwell not simply the personality but all that it represented in council with men like Goodwin and Owen. From first to last, I must keep before you, Independency has pursued not a dogma but a polity based on a gospel. Its interest has not been pure doctrine through a church so much as a true church through a gospel, a true church in a true state. It has been social rather than academic. And sometimes to its cost— to its peril at least in recent times; when the social enthusiasm around it kindles this side of its native genius by such a vehement affinity that the interest of its creative truth is in danger of neglect if only crowds are won by the preaching or philanthropy which this truth inspired. It has always had that sense of the real world which was so pre-eminent in Cromwell, and it has had the consequent temptation, when its dogmatic base was shaken or dissolved, of becoming the victim of that world. Its Anabaptist and popular strain is always ready to break out; and last century, in reaction from a debased and sectarian Calvinism, that strain made it too readily accept, along with Arminian universalism, the Arminian neglect of the Holy Spirit, and its reliance only on the content of the Word acting in an ethical and impressionist way on the soul. This in turn prepared us too quickly to echo in an amateur fashion the note of theological liberalism which sounded from Germany. When Independency does lose hold of a positive gospel it is easily affected by passing gales, by sentimental philosophy in its faith, by academic criticism in its creed, and by social reform in its works, owing to the very closeness of its contact with the public. Its gospel for the people has also to save it from the people. Cromwell had, what the enthusiasts and sectaries he broke from had not, an equally deep sense of the Christian Gospel, of the public situation, and of the historic boons of civilisation and the fruits of culture. His religion was theological, as Independency has always been, but it was not directed or dominated by the theologians, except where a theological issue comes to the front and the very existence of Christianity is involved. He did not aim at a theocracy. He insisted on the freedom of the state from the control of professional religion, as well as on the freedom of religion from the official state. If the word were allowed, he aimed at a thearchy rather than a theocracy, the monarchy of God in the nation without His vice-gerent of a Church. It was in such ways that the Anabaptist influences modified the Calvinism on which Independency stood. Robinson was a convinced Calvinist, qualified however by much fineness of nature, much humane culture, and much contact with the religion of the Low Countries. Independency represents Calvinism humanised by much personal experience of an Anabaptist intimacy and directness ; it represents Anabaptism annealed by failure, and set upon the positive base which Calvinism gave when it ceased to be doctrinaire, and its dogma was not made a public pedantry. Its religious experience was much more vivid, immediate, and individual than in Calvinism or Puritanism, but it drew enough from these to set it on a sure and steady foundation. It kept on solid, historic, and dogmatic ground, though it was not chiefly concerned with raising or guarding dogmatic fabrics upon it. It was kept concrete.; and it had the power, especially through Cromwell, to shed the fantastic, the hectic, the conventicular, the apocalyptic, while it retained a note personal, evangelical, and free.

I said a little ago that Independency was more

concerned with polity than dogma, and its interest
was not in pure doctrine through a church but in a
true church through a gospel. That is to say, its
type of religion had ceased to be medieval and was
so far modern in that it was psychological and
social. It was the religion of souls with a history
bred in a society. It was rooted in a positive and
experimental soil—in the evangelical experience,
and from there it grew. The Gospel was fixed, not
only as the keystone of a system but as a living
genetic centre. This shows again the Anabaptist
influence. It gave the theology a living soul. It
set it in motion with a personal thrill. It made
the theology passionate and paraenetic, as the pro-
jection and confession of a life created anew in the
Holy Spirit. Its treatises were conceived, delivered,
and published as sermons. Theology was not an
academic science which might be pursued by a
speculative calculus with comparative personal
indifference ; it was a transcript of personal faith,
developed in a living company of saints. Its
foundation was not metaphysical, but what would
now be called meta-historic. It reflected the
Christian psychology of a church that not only
believed but habitually lived on a world-faith.
The theology of Puritanism was Calvinism schol-
asticised at two removes, and it was as much below
Calvin as Calvinism was below Independency in

the matter of personal religion. It might be described by comparison as survey and specification. It was a piece of divine chartography, the result of a government survey by the Church's geodetic staff in the region of religious truth. The triangulation was well done from a fixed evangelical base. Truly there was life in the Church that produced it, but it was still life, sacred landscape in repose. There was no ferment, no stir or glow of growth, and no provision for growth. But the theology of Independency, Calvinistic as it was, was a different Calvinism from that and nearer its great source—different by all the lift, flush, and tumult of Anabaptism. It put soul upon the scene. There was wine in the bottles. There was sap in the veins. We are reminded of this when we recall that John Robinson's well-known words (to which I shall recur) about the Lord having yet more light and truth to break forth from His Holy Word were spoken by a very thorough Calvinist. But he was a Calvinist twice born. The machine became an organism. The system became vital. It was not laid out round its centre—it grew from its source. Theology (think of Owen and Goodwin) from being medieval and metaphysical became modern and psychological in spirit ; though the old forms remained, a new current was sent through them, and the old fittings were used for the new force.

Theology became capable of being preached,
because it was a living thing, a life's confession.
Like a great epic it was first lived.   It was the
reflex of an intelligence not only acute and incisive
but subtle, penetrative, and passionate.   Theological truth was not the deposit of a school's
thought but the register of the Church's intimate
experience of eternal things.   There is something
more than Shakespearean in the dramatic majesty
and passionate intimacy of some of Goodwin's
pages, because they apply genius to a region of the
soul above any that Shakespeare ever entered.
They not only tingle, they soar ; and they come
home with a beauty and poignancy of spiritual
truth which make them, ever after they are read,
ingredients in one's own spiritual life.   Some of
Goodwin's passages of practical application will
not only bear comparison with Jeremy Taylor, but
they touch and awe and stay us more, because
of their businesslike spiritual veracity and the absence of any suspicion of fine writing.   I may refer,
for instance, to his magnificent homiletic of *Election* and its unspeakable love in the eleventh and
nineteenth sermons expounding Ephesians ; to his
stately sermon to the House of Commons on *The
Great Interest of States and Kingdoms*; or to such
moving and imaginative thought as is made to
pass before us in the fourth chapter of the ninth

book of his treatise on the work of the Holy Spirit.
May I quote that ?   He there makes it a true mark
of regeneration that in our repentance we are less
concerned about our doom and misery, and more
about the dishonour done to God who is wounded
by it, and whose favour is more than life.

"Which sorrow, being for thy offence against
God, so much the more increaseth by how much
thou apprehendest he is pacified towards thee.
And though thy heart should not apprehend so
much, yet there are some relentings in it for offend-
ing Him whom thy soul loves. *So as, if now
the sentence of death were passed against thee, as at
the latter day, and thou wert out of hope, yet, at thy
doleful farewell from Him thou couldst find in thy
heart to down on thy knees and ask Him forgiveness
first for all the wrongs thou hast done Him.*"

I will say that the pathetic sublimity, the
moving grandeur of that is to me beyond all
measure.   Milton never made the sublime so tender
as that.   And the phrase of *thy doleful farewell
from Him*, set in such a picture, since first I read
it, has never ceased to glow in my memory like a
jewel five words long, and to vibrate there like a
motive of Schubert, or as certain tones still do of
Sarah Bernhardt and Charles Kean.

And as I have named Goodwin, the apostle and
high priest of our confession, I will quote one short

sentence from him which has a special bearing on
that living genetic manner of Christian truth which
I have noted as the mark left by Anabaptism on
Independent theology—that psychological quality
which makes theology the process and evolution in
living experience of its living gospel. He says at
the end of his brief premise to his *Exposition of
Ephesians* :—

"If Christian judgments be well and thoroughly
grounded in the doctrine of God's free grace and
eternal love and redemption through Jesus Christ
alone, and in the most spiritual inward operations
of God's Spirit, that will fence them against all
errors."

We have here one of many expressions of his
to the effect that a theology of Christian truth is a
living thing and not a closed system, a living reflex
of a corporate soul fructified by the germ of experienced grace. For that grace has not to be secured
in a scaffolding of extraneous philosophy but it
carries within itself and its nature its own expansive
power, its own organic form, and its own self-
corrective principle, subduing every thought to the
soul's organic obedience to its new creator Christ.
The Spirit is the living steward of the Holy Word.
And to that gospel of grace, as we are continually
sent forth from it, so we must continually return,
to adjust our compass and take our course. From

there go forth the organising surges which at once make our impulse and our law, which quicken faith and shape it, as we expand on all sides into the plerophory of Christian truth. It is more than our base, it is our source; and what issues there carries with it the free principle of its own form and its own career, whether in thought or polity.

The point I am pressing, as you perceive, is that, owing to the quick, immediate, and religious vitality which Anabaptism gave to our original Calvinism, our theology is not a fixed system we must accept but a gracious experience which we must declare, not the mould but the image of the Church's spiritual life. It therefore advances with it, but always by the power which makes a man a Christian and the Church the Church, the power of our regeneration in the grace, cross, resurrection, and Holy Spirit of Jesus Christ our Lord and Saviour. Rooted in that freedom we theologise as it compels. For it is the compulsion of a new freedom and not of a new scheme, of a final gospel and not a fixed law. We believe by the divine must of that founded liberty, and certainly we do not believe as we please. We think most freely when our first concern is to be bound to our freedom in redemption.

Thus Independency, though mothered by Anabaptism, was not fathered by it. It was not like Anabaptism non-resistant. It was not neutral to government. It was not apocalyptic. It was organic with the national life. But it was more concerned with a historic and national evolution than with a social programme. Plenty of Anabaptist features were found among the Independents, plenty tend from time to time to grow up among them. To-day many, like Troeltsch, would find Sebastian Franck more to their mind than Luther, others are more at home with the Quakers than with Calvin. But they do not represent the essence, idea, and genius of Independency; which truly was not itself when the dogmatic interest was supreme, yet also on the other hand belies its whole history when either spiritual or social interests produce dogmatic indifference. It is not then Cromwell's, Goodwin's, Robinson's Independency. It has lost its apostolic succession, its evangelical base, its regenerate atmosphere. It is true neither to Calvin its father nor to Anabaptism its mother. It has more of the note of that continental Socinianism which is so remarkably absent from the whole development of Independency till quite a late and decadent stage. The Antitrinitarian views of the Socini which took such a hold of the Continent in the sixteenth and seventeenth centuries found but

sporadic footing in England either then or for long
after. Unitarianism did not become a community
until after the Restoration, and then often in the
modified form of Arianism. Independency did not
live for dogma but it could not live without it,
and it ceases to be Independency without it. It
ceases to be a church. It becomes but religious
clubland. It held to a dogmatic base, but without
dogmatic compulsion, or a unitary institutional
church exercising such compulsion. It claimed the
right to emit from time to time a declaration of
belief, which, however, was to be common and
characteristic, and not subscriptional or coercive
at the hands either of Church or of State. The
State was to be Christian, but not by virtue of
the establishment of an organised Church. The
Church was to be Christian but not by the
establishment of an organised creed. Both were
to be Christian on the level base of a common
Christianity, which meant an experienced faith of
forgiveness through the death of the Son of God.
Christianity, in a nation of such men, was to be established only by public conduct according thereto,
and the manifested ethic of a life hidden with *such*
a Christ in God. They might fall into a variety of
churches, but God would save His truth in freedom,
if it is His freedom, founded on obedience to His
law, and especially on the prime obedience which is

faith in His grace.   So that Independency stood for
moral rigour and dogmatic freedom on a genial evangelical base.   Liberty was always on a basis of the
divine authority of grace and not the mere exercise
of natural right.   It was on the authority and in
the power of a changeless Christianity.   Here was
introduced the distinction, which we shall note
more particularly later as associated with Baxter,
between fundamentals and circumstantials.   And
the fundamental thing, which was the condition
of all liberty within a church, was personal faith
in a forgiven reconciliation through Christ's death.
That was so at our source, and always it must be
so, if we are not to be scattered upon all waters
by all winds.   Coercion was to be applied only in
the matter of conduct, ' the coercion by a serious
majority of a lax minority.'   And Troeltsch sums
up the features of the Independent programme on
this base, ' Autonomy of religion and Church,
political self-government by the democracy, the
moral severity of Puritanism, tempered by spirituality and culture, justice made popular and
courts accessible, the ruler to exercise moral and
religious vigilance.'   All of which, along with other
features, made the experiment the first really
Christian state in history—much more Christian
than Geneva, though it was Geneva that made it
possible.   ' The rule of Cromwell's saints is the

turning-point in the history of Protestantism. It is the last religious movement of a people, the end of the wars of religion, the point of departure for the modern world.' Social forces, political and economic, were here freed from religious control, and made independent of direct connection with spiritual developments. They became rational in base and standard. Ethic, while Christian in ideal and temper, was put on a natural footing. Toleration was established in principle in the public realm, and it was soon to claim a more questionable place as an unlimited comprehension within the Church. Independency became the parent, as it has since been the protagonist, of civil liberalism. It believed that every soul, being created by a Christian God for redemption, was Christian in its destiny; that it had therefore a right to Christian liberties, and especially the right to be free for everything necessary to the exercise and growth of a Christian personality in society. This Christian personality was the greatest thing in man, the greatest asset of a people, the greatest interest of all policy. It was the greatest stake that any man could hold in the country; and it made the peer's real stake just equal to the peasant's in a society thus moralised. Each could stake in the nation no more than the soul or person, for whose uses all property or place was valuable. To evolve this moral soul was the object of society and its laws, the purpose and course of God's world.

Thus an Independency based on the soul's predestination and nurtured in a spiritual experience has been carried from the predestination of some to the predestination of all. It has gradually replaced a predestination by power with a predestination by love. It made a reality of our predestination *in Christ* and the Christ of Humanity. Such religious views affected greatly the purpose and the range of predestination, and they were bound to have political effect. And the political effect was the liberalism of the modern world. True it has gone far from its base in very many cases, and forgotten or disowned the Bethel where God gave it its career. The assurance of the saint's soul has become the mere individualism of the natural ego, or the mere altruism which is sympathetically concerned for other egos, apart from a purpose of God with either. As a German puts it in his cumbrous but effective way, ' The subjectivity of religious Independency becomes the subjectivism of the modern citizen.' Inwardness becomes egoism. The political interest has often submerged the ecclesiastical, and even the evangelical. So that ardent Nonconformists and politicians, of culture in some kinds, may be found denouncing and despising that great creator of the liberties of the modern world, Calvin, in a way that shows how completely historic knowledge and spiritual insight have been eclipsed by the mere order of the parliamentary day.

But modern Independents are apt to be driven into politics, first, because they have nothing in their church life to satisfy the political instinct which is so strong both in human nature and in their own tradition. They have no part in a great organisation that can do things, like a connectional church. This is the case of many a village pastor who eats his soul out in a poverty of practical opportunity, if he do not secularise it in local politics. And, in the next place, because they are led to think that Christianity has a direct political ethic; whereas its direct action is to create a moral soul, and thus a social or national ethos, which then creates the public ethic. It is too easy on both sides to identify one political form with ethical Christianity. There is no political form directly given by Christianity. Christ laid down no political ethic. He gave no theory or structure of the true State, with a divine right. Yet the Christian gospel does involve an ethic, social in its very nature as a kingdom, which contributes much and powerfully, and at the far end decisively, to political ethic. Christianity has much to do with politics. But it does not follow that it must do it directly, through the Church, or especially the Church's ministers. It is a fallacy, which misleads many, to suppose that Christianity is a divine republication of the *lex naturae* in a spiritualised form which is a divine charter of natural rights. That way lies much spiritual legalism, and the capture of the free churches by a subtle erastianism.

It has been the misfortune of Independency to have suffered in greater or less measure from the liberalism it created, whether political or theological. Not indeed that it should be less liberal, but that it should be less the victim of its liberalism. It has sometimes cared more for freedom than for the truth that makes free—even to calling the care for such truth reactionary.[1] It has in cases become more interested in liberalism than in the Gospel. It has often at least acquired insight into the one more keenly and deeply than into the other. More of its members understand election issues than gauge the Lord's controversy. The old religious individualism, reared under our Election by

---

[1] First the truth then the freedom, says Harnack, replying to Jatho, "Science [in a University] indeed not only may but must ask and pursue truth regardless of the soul or its salvation; but the Churches have not only the right but the duty to maintain the distinctive and mighty thing in Christianity as it emerges from the original fabric and the history in its train. And in this effort they are supported by true historical science. But to say that between the letter of a creed and sheer subjectivism the Churches have no third course, is a statement easily dismissed."

God, has given way to secular constructions of
liberty, which were but the natural man enlarged,
mere democratic ideas of equality, and a genial
notion of fraternity. The communion of saints is
practically meaningless to many who are devotees
of the brotherhood of man. The undoubted right
to live, the sound right to the means of living,
takes the place once held by the duty of glorifying
God in life and life's occasions. With the retreat
of the idea of predestination has come the assertion
of a free career. And we have liberalism rather
co-existing with Christian principles in the same
mind than flowing from them. Often it is no more
than theistic, often not that. It rests (it has been
said) on a notion that the human units, equipped
with certain rights and qualities, exist in a natural
and pre-established harmony which we must make
actual, a harmony like that of the physical atoms
in the mechanical philosophy. The dogmatic
base, from which this public liberalism first sprang,
is replaced by a natural base, which Christianity
does not create but only reissues in a new edition,
permissu superiorum. The law of nature is not
based on the Bible, but on natural religion of the
Stoic fur; the Bible is interpreted by that rather
than that by the Bible; and everything in the Bible,
or even in the Gospel, which traverses that or
limits it is ruled out. That is to say, liberalism

ceases to be a religious principle and becomes a
social philosophy.   It is less a Christian product
than a political ethic held by Christian men.
But it captures religious thought as well as rules
political; and it pervades faith, as I have said, with
a subtle erastianism, which saturates and weakens
even the grounds of liberationist protest against
the erastianism of the obvious kind.   The welfare
of the individual or of the people not only is
pursued, as it must be, but it takes the place once
held by the glory and purpose of God; and society
is organised for the one without much apparent
reference to the other.   Hobbes, Locke, and Adam
Smith have, to an extent which I do not venture to
measure, taken the place of Cromwell or Milton—
except on religious platforms.   The inviolable freedom of the individual takes the place once kept for
his absolute dependence and obedience before God.

All this is the inevitable consequence of the
popularising of a great principle.   Its facilities are
prized by more than appreciate its fountain or its
force.   It is not for a moment said here that the
faith which made liberalism is extinguished by
its creature.   But it is certainly obscured or postponed in the case of many of the protagonists
(especially the younger) of our public life.   And
no one would say that it was as operative in the
recent decapitation of the peers as it was in the

I

decapitation of the king. It is not easy to see how it could be. If such things are done by religion, it needs a very powerful and sublime type of religion. It required ' the last of the Heroisms ' in its time. And that is impossible at this moment, amid the unsettlement or collapse of positive faith. Liberalism in politics has the solemn note taken out of it by liberalism in belief, by the theological liberalism or nescience which kills a generous theology.

Here also, in the matter of belief, native and individual liberty takes the place of divine vocation; which was not simply a release but a redemption and a regeneration. We have seen how predestination, from being a theological doctrine in Puritanism, became in Independency a personal certainty of immense religious enthusiasm, and that largely through Anabaptism, through an obsession by the Spirit at the cost of the Word. But this meant in due course that faith became mere inspiration, which went on to take the lead of revelation. The Bible ceased to be read only in the light of an inspiration which created it, and it was brought to the bar of the inspiration it creates. It was read, not in the light of a revelation given once for all, but of one which flashes in momentarily, impulsively, even explosively, upon the pious soul. That momentary illumination might or might not agree with the

Bible. Mostly at first it did, because the personal inspiration was kindled by it. But at least it put the Bible in a new position, and one strange to most of the Reformers. It did not interpret it by a principle drawn from it, but by the light it struck on the soul—as if to-day the Christian *littérateur* were a sounder expositor of Christianity than the saintly theologian. So also the Church, ceasing to be a miraculous institution which God made once for all, became a voluntary corporation which man makes from time to time in his Christian freedom and democratic faith, for worship and work. Instead of one church and one truth there were churches many and views many. Hence the relation of Church to State became a question of quite a new colour. Is it to be parity, preference, or neutrality, the establishment of all churches, of one, or of none ? Both Lutherism and Calvinism have been overruled by the Anabaptism they persecuted. Their objective gospel fell a prey to subjective illumination. People believed only what they felt did them good, and as far as they felt it. They were impatient of everything but edification, especially impatient of talk about redemption or regeneration. And then the subjectivism moved from the religious to the rational. The supernatural spiritualism of Münzer, Karlstadt, and Schwenkfeld passed into the natural and rational of Franck, Denk,

Weigel, and modern liberalism. The illumination of the Quaker became the rationalism of the Aufklärung. The inner light took a harder and more natural phase.

And now the great struggle of our time in this region must be to recover for the Bible Word the positive and final authority it has parted with to natural religion in more or less rarefied forms. To the Bible as the Reformers read it we can never, indeed, return. And the Bible of the illuminationist is at best an edification, it is not a revelation. Means must be found of placing the Gospel, which is the Bible's core and life, in the place which the infallible Book once held ; and of securing it in authority over the popular subjectivism by which the churches must fade into spiritual egoism, religious sentiment, rational anarchy, and moral impotence. A theology of the great fact must replace a theology of the mere spirit of Christ. That is the task of modern evangelicalism, to rescue from the Bible its positive and final gospel.

LECTURE VI

PARTICULAR ANABAPTIST FEATURES IN
INDEPENDENCY

I HAVE been trying to impress upon you that the element differentiating Independency from Puritanism and Presbyterianism was neither theological on the one hand, nor ecclesiastical on the other. It was neither dogma nor polity in chief. It was a religious difference—spiritual and social, enthusiastic and democratic. It was the element that went to its extreme, on the one side, in the Quakers, and, on the other, in the Levellers. It was, in a word, the Anabaptist element, with its supremacy of the inner light and of the direct note, of the unwritten word and the popular rule. We are well provided with histories of English Nonconformity.[1] But they are apt to leave us too insular. They do not *place* Independency in the context of the great Church, nor do they always grasp its true and creative work for the modern State throughout the West. It is provincial Christianity still, with a certain patois, as dear as the accent of a village

[1] Mr. H. Clark's is the latest, and in some ways the best.

Bethel, but yet a patois. Even when we are made to feel our spiritual work for the nation we do not realise it for history. And we do not always reflect the national note. We do not envisage Independency in the whole context of the Reformation age, or of the world's course either backwards or forward. We treat it as coming too directly from the Reformers, or rising too wholly indigenous to England, or as too wholly confined in its effects to England or America. And indeed the whole purview of the historians of Independency has regarded it too much as a piece of English history, or the history of English religion, and too little as an organic part of the spiritual history of the West. The function of Holland in particular, as our chief nexus with continental influences, is not grasped. It is too accidental with us, as if it were no more than a city of refuge, where we learned nothing and forgot nothing, instead of a spiritual school, where the masters spoke the word of the martyred saints, and Ana-baptism taught as one risen from the dead.

Forgive me if I pick up previous allusions to this newer point and extend them. The influence of Holland on Puritanism had already been very great. Its type of Protestantism was Calvinist. But it was Calvinism sanctified by the great struggle with Spain, and taught public wisdom by the

Cromwell of Holland, William the Silent. Our second Cromwell owed much to the first. Part of that public and reasonable wisdom was toleration. And in Holland therefore the fugitive Anabaptists (chiefly known there as Mennonites) had their liberty and their influence. What I have not said already refers first to the immense number of English who lived in Holland during the seventeenth century, either permanently, as merchants, or for a time in military service. They were much impressed with the ideas of the Dutch Republic, which, in all the interests of civilisation, was then the centre of Europe, and probably two centuries ahead of the rest of it. And I refer, secondly, to the great influence of the Dutch upon our Puritanism through the refugees from Spanish rule, who had flooded the eastern counties with a type of Protestant faith specially high-minded, seeing that they came not for gain but for religious liberty, seeking in England that which Englishmen before long had to seek still farther west in America. It is computed that no fewer than fifty to seventy thousand such heads of families sought shelter in England at this time, and made the whole region between Lincoln, Norwich, and London the chief seat of a Puritanism whose impress is still conspicuous there. The influence continued, and was increased, when the tide turned, when William had beaten Alva, set up the tolerance of the Dutch Republic, and opened a refuge for the English Separatists (who, being plebeian, were treated with so much more rigour than the middle-class Puritans). These Separatists were naturally much drawn to the Mennonites, who were indeed, by their refugees, in all probability the real begetters of Brownism. At any rate more than half the population of Norwich, where Browne had charge of a congregation, was composed of fugitives from the Low Countries engaged in manufactures, as Douglas Campbell points out in his fascinating book, *The Puritan in Holland, England, and America* (two vols., Harper, 1893). It was inevitable that the rudiments of English Independency should be much influenced, if not indeed aroused, by these highly spiritual people, with their faith in the local church, their conception of the Church as a voluntary corporation instead of an imperative institution, and their principle of the separation of Church and State.

It is quite true, nevertheless, that Independency was not simply Anabaptism in resurrection. That would be more true of the Baptists and the Quakers. Fox expounded Mennonitism,[1] and Penn had a

---

[1] I think Mr. Clark, in his interesting and valuable *History of Nonconformity*, is mistaken when he says (i. p. 361) : ' If ever a movement was founded by one man Quakerism was.' He is in like error about his insulation of Wicliff from the mentality of the medieval Church.

Dutch mother. The extremest tenets of Anabaptism, however, Independency shook off when
its lesson had been learned. But if Independency
(always including the Baptists) alone gave true
effect to the material principle of Reformation
faith, and won for it a form congenial to its own
inner nature it was (ironically enough) by the aid of
those Anabaptist inspirations which the Reformers
sought to extirpate.

There are three features in Independency which
we may examine in this light.

1. Its theological liberty ;
2. Its inwardness and spirituality, what would
by some be called its subjectivity ;
3. Its chiliastic element.

1. Independency took faith in popular earnest.
The Reformation was not a popular movement.
It promised to be, but it was not. By its definition
of faith it should have been, but it was not. Nor
was it so religious in the mass as in its greatest
leaders. It was too easily captured by the ruling
political powers. This may have been a historical
necessity. Rome, as I have already said, might
have regained the whole field but for the German
princes who were secured at such a cost. But this
only means that another movement had to supple-
ment the practical work of the first Reformers for
their own original idea, and give it its native scope.

It was in England that this justice was done to faith, and it was done by the aid of that power latent in Anabaptism which the Reformers renounced.

There are, in a matter so great as faith, so deep, high, and wide, three features, with three far-reaching effects. There is its theology, its sociology, and its religion; its effect on truth as a doctrine, on society as a church, and on the soul as a power and experience.

(1) In respect of the first, its teaching, we have seen that Independency did not have dogma for a prime interest. It did not cultivate schools of scientific doctrine. It did not do so much there as even German Anabaptism did. It was English not only in that it was free and self-governing, but also in that it was selective and cautious in what it took from the Anabaptist creed. It was not affected, except sporadically, by the Unitarian aspects of the inner light and the present Word. In so far as it was theological it was so either systematically, in the way of borrowing from Calvin (with Owen and Robinson), or experimentally, in making Christianity the plastic experience of Christ's atoning redemption (Cromwell and Goodwin). And it is in keeping with this priority of interests other than dogmatic, that Independency has been associated with so much theological

liberty upon the evangelical base, not of Biblicism, but of Biblical positivism.

We should be very clear that however theological the tradition of Independency has been, especially in the decadence of the eighteenth century, its genius or its *metier* has never been theological science, but theological positivity. It has run to preaching rather than thought; and the defect of this quality is that it stands the impressionist risk of succumbing to a preaching personality at the cost of preached truth. Its note has not been theological system but theological footing, not an ordered knowledge of divine procedure but an experienced certainty of divine redemption. Hence its freedom is not the unchartered liberty of science, the culture of absolutely disinterested truth (for saving truth can never be disinterested); nor is it the application within the Church of the unlimited toleration which becomes the State. But it is such liberty of thought as grows from an evangelical foundation, consists with apostolic finality, and unfolds the wealth of that new infinite world. It is not made of Adullamites but Israelites. And it is not, by its genius or history, a theological Alsatia among the other churches, which would mean ceasing to be a church at all, and becoming a popular laboratory of religious inquiry, which would turn a good church into a bad university.

(2) It was upon the second and third elements of faith that Independency chiefly seized. It drew the true inference from Reformation faith in respect of church polity. It strove to organise the Church on the basis of the personal faith of the community, on its confession of the Gospel, and not of a system or creed. Its church was not an institution but a corporation. It began where Christianity began, in a divinely given fact of gospel, and not in an analysis of the religious consciousness. And it would give faith scope to organise itself by its native powers and affinities, without such an arrest and deflection as the Roman Empire laid upon faith's youth in the Catholic Church. It may be observed that this plastic action of faith still goes on in the movement for the federation of the free churches, which seeks to realise the unity of the great Church, not by resumption under a miracu-lous historic institution, but by free combination as voluntary corporations.

(3) So we come to faith as an experience, faith in its inwardness.

2. The most distinctive feature of Independency, as it came to itself, arose in connection with faith's action upon the soul. It was its inwardness, its spirituality, its prophetism, which involved free address both to man in preaching and to God in prayer. This subjectivity has been among the

most persistent of all its features, even leading to
unhappy extremes, especially in the exclusion of
anything liturgical in worship, in the exaggeration,
not to say idolatry, of preaching, and the temptation even to sacrifice Gospel truth to the preaching
aptitude and its prompt success with crowds. It
has not always escaped the democratic peril which
postpones the love of truth to the culture of individuality, and is more interested in temperament
than in salvation.

The first Independents, it has been remarked,
were known as ' believers ' ; in Cromwell's time
they had come to call themselves ' saints.' The
Ironside army was the army of the saints. It is
a pity the word has fallen into disuse, for it
expresses a great thing both historically and
experimentally. It certainly indicates the differ-
entia which gave Independency its own triumphant
line. It expressed the fact that faith was so
inward, spiritual, ardent, and personal that it
became inspiration. Independency became the
religion of prophetism. Like the old prophets it
cherished dreams and programmes which never
were, or could be, realised ; but these only covered
with a temporary hull the real, new, and vital power
that emerged. It is as easy to despise the chiliasts
and sectaries that haunted the precincts of the
Commonwealth as to ridicule the poor Anabaptists

of an earlier day abroad. But ridicule and contempt are mostly misplaced, except as Christ spent
them on the 'leaven of that fox Herod,' *i.e.* for
pretentious incompetency in high place. They are
a mistake in connection with deep spiritual movements. And there is a great deal in the chiliasts
and fantastics of the seventeenth century which
makes a most valuable parallel and commentary on
the prophets of Israel, their method and *entourage,*
as well as on the prophets of the first Church,
till these last were put to school under the evangelical control that Paul expended so wisely on
his Corinthians. The root of the great matter still
worked mightily in these strange exponents of the
Spirit. And the fanatics of Independency had
that in them which, when anchored on the historic gospel, purified by action, and schooled by
the genius of great realists like Cromwell, made
Independency the world-power in history which
Puritanism was too theological to become.

Faith turns here to be an inspiration instead of
a mere assent, or even a conviction—an inspiration
for the Christian layman instead of capital for the
official theologian. That was the principle which
Anabaptism contributed to English religion through
Independency—the living Spirit, separate from the
world but intimate with the Word ; yet not merely
alongside the historic Word, and not above it. Even

Milton wandered into saying that it was above it, for poetic genius chafes at history as restraint, and has more affinity for a free Spirit than a saving Word. Milton sacrificed Word to Spirit and it made an Arian of him. But Independency meant the living Spirit on the foundation of the historic Word, and issuing through it. And the historic Word was not Christ as the mystic Logos of spiritual Humanity, sparkling in every soul (which was the Quaker line), but Christ as the saving action and grace of God for a new Humanity at an eternal and creative point in history for our reconciliation and regeneration. Such liberty, on such fixity, was the note of Independency when it settled from its early ferment and found its true soul. Out of all the fanciful forms it took in its vagrant youth this emerges as the Independent principle of the classic time—the realisation of the soul's redeemed life in its true, personal, and predestined spirituality, the immediacy of that life, the autonomy of it, the tremendous, overwhelming, incomparable reality of it, and, above all, of the revelation which created it. Bunyan and Cromwell are at one as representatives of this genius of faith, this promotion of Puritan conviction to Independent enthusiasm, this exaltation, this moralising, of the conviction of truth to become the conviction of sin and grace. The self-occupation

with which the *Pilgrim's Progress* has been charged
is the first stage of self-conquest ; and it is a far
higher thing than the self-engrossment of so many
geniuses who have even preached the altruistic
gospel. I need but name Schopenhauer, to say
nothing of a cloud of those musicians whom he
regarded as the apostles of the only gospel left us ;
which, after all, like everything æsthetic, is a mere
lenitive to the soul that tastes a dismal fate. The
whole of that Commonwealth ferment of enthusiasm
was so profoundly based on the faith and sense of
the new creation that it was full also of the sense
of a quite new social world which through it should
come to pass. And it did come to pass, though
(here again like old prophecy) not in the shape
of their often fantastic dreams. The central principles of Independency did remake history. They
made the modern political world. They made a
world-power of the liberty which Holland had only
made a world example. And they did it on the
moral basis of a conscience regenerate in Christ alone.

This enthusiasm of the inner light went far in
some cases to dissolve Protestant, and even
Christian, belief ; especially in the absence of a
real dogmatic interest, or a guiding declaration of
Church belief. The fine and gifted Unitarian,
John James Taylor, in his *History of Religion in*

England (p. 165, second edition), says of the
Quakers, among whom, as among the Anabaptists,
all the modern heresies seem then to have had
much course : ' It may be questioned whether
their principle of renouncing all external guidance,
and of throwing each man on the suggestions of
his own spirit, might not issue, if it were tried
on a large scale, in raising up at last, from the
sheer necessity of the case, some great sacerdotal
authority to guide the aimless and fluctuating mass
of minds. Such a sense of intellectual helplessness
as would probably result is the very condition
which the Catholic priesthood would most desire
for the promotion of its own views.' Many fine
things were said, true so far as they went, and
said with special force at such a time. They were
said with much more force and relevancy than they
would have now, when we have learned their lesson,
and it has awakened us to a different need. This,
for instance, from Francis White (1649) : ' Religion
is not a name but a thing, not a form but a power,
not a notion but a substance divine. Religion is
properly that inward power in the soul of a man
whereby he believeth and is bound to God in
righteousness and holiness. So much of this power
as a man hath so much religion. Where there is
none of this power there is no religion.'

But Christianity is not mere religion and not mere

K

inwardness, it is faith; and when mere inwardness becomes the religion of an atomic mass, when it is enthroned by their spiritual imagination above all that is outward or historic, there is no limit to the fantasies it may produce. It acquires all the vices of the religious autodidact. It becomes indifferent to the providential powers and personalities of the past; and, being proudly ignorant of historic movements and thought, it treats its own finds as original discoveries, without knowing how long they have been dead and buried and transcended. Mysticism always tends to ignore active history and social faith. It is immediate and individualist. It knows but of the action of the Spirit, not of a Church of the Spirit. It tends to become a temerarious spiritualism. Its history becomes the quest of spiritual adventure instead of a discovery of the unsearchable riches of Christ. It sails by no star, and it boxes the compass of the creeds, till it is captured drifting, and towed into port by a cruiser of Rome. Christ becomes but a prophet, who met the prophet's usual fate at Jerusalem. He was not spiritual enough to be the prophet for our day that He was for His own. He was a passing symbol of the Spirit and not God's last Word. All Bible history is but a spiritual allegory for use in edification. The voices and suggestions that shake unlettered peasants to-day

may be of equal value with the Word that came
to elect Apostles. The amateur theologies of the
Bible-reader are on the same footing of authority
as those of the apostolic Bible-maker. Both are
but tentative interpretations of some ineffable
experience. The Spirit in the present takes pre-
cedence of any Word from the past.

We are familiar still with this anti-apostolic succession. It is mentioned here that we may remind
ourselves how, at the outset, Independency had to
work its way through such things to come to its
own (as Christianity itself, in a like ferment, had
to find itself through the chaos of Gnosticism);
how it had to clarify and settle; how it had
to gather in upon a historic gospel in order
to secure its own historic place and influence.
All these recurrent eccentricities and abuses
of freedom are but extreme expressions of that
principle of inwardness which is so precious but
by itself so futile, a strand so precious but so
precarious as a rope. They show how the religious
subjectivity, which in the original Brownist Independency was used but as a base for the constitutional autonomy of the single Church, became in
the next stage of the sectaries the principle of faith
and the spiritual life altogether. And they prepare
us for the next stage after that, when they had to
be taken in hand, and reduced to their proper and

useful place under some principle and gospel more objective and positive, able to quell the despotism of a clergy or a church, and yet to erect a living centre both of power and guidance for the free Church and the free soul.

3. The third feature of Independency was its chiliasm. And it is continuous to-day in our inveterate and optimistic belief in the imminence of the great and final social age. We have cast off the apocalyptic hulls of the Commonwealth period, and we are clothed in economics and a right mind. But the passion remains. We do not expect to see Christ descend in clouds, but we are very sure of a great and revolutionary Christian future for man-kind not indefinitely remote. Some are even surer of a Christian future than of the Christian past. But on the whole it is the sign of a great and not a decadent age. Some of the most powerful and pregnant periods in history have teemed with these ideas, which, however Utopian their forms, have an optimism which belongs to the greatness of faith. It has been happily said that the chiliastic form in such cases is but the minute-hand upon the dial of time ; while it is the hours that we must chiefly regard. We cannot read a great believer, saint, and theologian like Goodwin, with his public mind, without feeling how deep in him and his time was the presentiment of a huge new departure in

the world's history.[1] Nor can we look back from
now to then without feeling how just the soul of
that boding was. God tells His secrets, if not always
His tactics, to His servants these prophets. They
have the intuition and the inspiration, and the
secret, if not the machinery, of a great emancipation for the world. Their other worldliness was
also a mighty inner-worldliness. They had *l'au delà
interieur*. They feel the thrill along the line of God.
They forefeel the stirrings of the great democratic
age, charged equally with possibility and with peril
for the kingdom of God, but never out of His long
leash. For was not the foundation of the people's
sovereignty the self-government, under Him, of His
own people in a Church ? To this they were always
driven back. For, though a Milton or a Roger
Williams came to a pitch that they would have
every man serve God by himself alone, without any
church at all, these were extremes due to the situation of the time. And in so far as they were but
ideas they were not adopted as the Independent
principle ; which after all arose to lay prime stress
not on the independency of either the member
or the minister but of the Church ; and on the
autonomy of the Church as the moral and spiritual sanative for the sovereignty of the people
always.

[1] See especially his sermon to the House of Commons.

It was not therefore the Reformation that put
an actual end to medievalism but Anabaptism, as
Troeltsch says. And it did so, not by itself—by
itself it was an ineffectual thing—but by the share
it had in creating the positive Independency which
changed the political history of the West and the
future. Medievalism did not end, therefore, till
the fruits of the English Revolution were secured
for good in the affairs of civilised nations. This
was indeed the watershed of two worlds for both
Church and State. The State became neutral to
the Church, though not to religion. The Church
ceased to be miraculous as an institution, though it
did not cease to be, in its nature, as miraculous as
grace, or the action of its Holy Spirit. Church and
State thus became separate, and each therefore
more free to be itself for the benefit of the other.
Organised religion sat more loosely to civilisation—
to the great increase of their mutual influence. The
one Christian life was recognised as growing into
a great variety of types. And the outcome of that
has been the end of one imperial Church and the
promise of a great federated Church. Collaterally
there has come the downfall of one grand dogmatic
system, and the cessation even of such an ideal.
There is no infallible system. System is not the
manner of the soul's relation to God. Revelation
has ceased to be primarily a thing of proposition

and statement, a scheme of intellectual truth, a
piece of knowledge in the noetic sense of that word.
It has therefore dropped the ambition of intellectual
unity as a postulate, and it courts it only in a
scientific way as a product and an approximation.
A system of truth can no more command the whole
of life on its modern scale. So also vanishes
the idea of State and Church as two aspects or
organs of one religious civilisation in a parity.
They have each a different origin, spirit, and
genius, close as their relations may be. They are
not two verbs with one nominative, two actions
of the same subject, two functions of one body.
The new era meant a variety of different beliefs
and communities, with the free right of each to
convert itself from a minority to a majority.
And, as a great unitary and imperial Church
became impossible, so also fell the idea of civilisation as one Empire of the old centralised
type. Imperialism, so far as it exists at all, must
exist by free federation, through ties of blood,
tradition, and sentiment, deeper, more flexible,
and yet more tenacious than organisation from
a despotic centre. In State as in Church the
great unities become those of action of spirit,
of faith, of sympathy; the ties of a common
country, or a common humanity, or a common
and experienced gospel, within which there is

much variety of life and entire freedom of conscience.

To have been the prime agent in the achievement
of such results is the chief glory of evangelical
Independency and the revolution it created.
Before the days of either the Illumination or the
French Revolution this creative idea was afloat
and at work upon the political world. And within
the Church these Anabaptist principles destroyed
the scholasticism of decadent Protestantism, the
Indian summer of medievalism in seventeenth-
century orthodoxy, and they opened the kingdom
of heaven to all hearty believers.

Outwardly the Independency that gave birth to
these transforming powers died in the act. After
the Commonwealth and the Revolution it ceased
to be a world power, or a power in the great Church.
It became isolated even within the insularity of
England. It had revolutionised the policy of the
world, but failed as a polity to convert England
and become a constitutional majority. It had
failed to organise the State upon its model of absolute freedom in the Church. The hasty attempt to
transfer the idea of religious autonomy directly to
political affairs came to grief in anarchy; for the
one had an authority latent in it and the other
had not. The failure was not the fault of the

idea but the vice of the time. Cromwell himself realised that. England was not far enough advanced morally to accept by a majority the principles forced on it by the army of a moral minority. And Cromwell could not secure the liberty he had set on its deathless way. Step by step he had to restore the old forms, as he could not destroy the nation's fear of a freedom established by force. The Puritans were not many, and the Independents were fewer still. The army was a ' vigorous dwarf,' which could not overcome the lazy good nature of the English giant. It was the army not the nation that slew the king; and the nation replaced him by another king. But a new world was begun nevertheless with England's lead. Even Tiberius and Caligula could not extinguish the spirit of Caesar, or quench the world hegemony of Rome; the genius of Caesar took new life in the Church of Rome. And so here. The Commonwealth idea could never retire from history. But it had to fashion, through time and experiment, its own political form. Freedom does not mean the same thing in religion as in politics. It has different postulates in each case, and a different ethic. A State polity cannot rest on Christian ethic till the State is composed of regenerated Christian men. And the only thing that can make public freedom safe at last is its control by the freedom of the soul in its most private, intimate, and final relation with God in Christ. The development of freedom is a slow process of adjusting the law of natural society to the Christian idea, and securing permanence for the cohesive instincts of human nature by the supernatural unity of its re-creation in the Son of God.

LECTURE VII

THE LIMITS AND DANGERS OF THE ANABAPTIST
ELEMENT IN INDEPENDENCY

I HAVE said that the failure of Independency in
the Commonwealth was really a premature triumph,
and was due to the vices of England rather than
the nature of the experiment. At least modern
England had been founded by it, especially her
commerce and her sea power. And the idea of
the sovereign people had been planted never again
to wither, though for long to grow but slowly.
What had secured the triumph was the Anabaptist affinity in Calvinism, its prophetism, that
side of predestination which insulates the single
soul in direct dependence on God, casts it, as even
Calvin did not, upon its immediate experiences, at
the cost perhaps of history and tradition (including
often Scripture), and develops the inner light with
its revelation straight from God, too regardless
sometimes of mediation by the past. It was on the
strength of this inner and individual inspiration
that Cromwell presented himself as God's chosen
ruler; and he appealed to men who believed too

much in such messages to challenge his claim
when made with such inward and outward power.
It was thus that he at once crowned Anabaptism
in the success, and ended it in the collapse, of
his experiment. And, apart from Cromwell, this
sufficiency of the inner light, this exaggeration of
one side of predestination, was tending to destroy
the other element of Calvinism—the solidarity of
the community, resting upon an objective Word,
positive, creative, and historic. Cromwell himself
had to fall back on this feature for his definition
of the Christians who were to have the freedom of
Church and State. And that was but one of the
signs how much practical men felt the need of a
definite base and an objective control for the ultra-
spiritualism and rationalism which ran riot then
in the name of the Spirit's liberty. To-day in like
manner we speak of the spirit of Christ, which
may mean no more than a theological Agnosticism
or indifference, sentimentally or ethically Christlike ;
and we need a similar objective control. Cromwell
could not impose on England or its Church that
positive faith in which he found his own footing,
and therefore he could not save his programme for
want of the condition that works it. Anabaptism, detached from an evangelical base, ended
in sentimental deism or rationalist mysticism, in a
humane unitarianism or such a humane spiritualism

as forms the note of much current religion.   And
it always must do so if it do not take its rise and
stand in a historic revelation appropriated in evangelical experience.   Mysticism we must have if
we are to have Christianity ; but it must be the
mysticism of history and not simply of the soul,
the mystery of God manifest in the flesh and not of
the soul on God's breast.   The notable point is that
spiritualism became effective and valuable only in
England, and only on a predestinarian and evangelical base.   And even in England it was ready to
fail, and it took the power of a very Cromwell to
save it, when the predestinarian subjectivity was
severed from the evangelical base, and the spiritualist egoism broke loose from a positive revelation.
The Church dissolves, and its effect on freedom is
lost for the State, when it ceases to be evangelical
in the great apostolic and Reformation sense of
being regenerate by the cross of the risen Christ.

This unchartered spiritualism had dissolved a
historic Church, and it was on the point of dissolving the historic State, had Cromwell not taken it
in hand, and used it to establish a dictatorship.
That only showed how essential a historic and
continuous constitution was, and how that constitution in English history could wear none but
the monarchical form.   In Church, as in State, religious republicanism had failed for the hour, both

in its aristocratic or presbyterian form, and in its
democratic or independent.   Both reverted to the
principle of monarchy, personal in Cromwell,
constitutional in William III.   But it was monarchy
now and for ever elective by the sovereign people.
That was the revolution made for good and all by
Independency, in spite of its first hasty error in
transferring to the masses of the England that then
was the constitution of its picked people in a
church.   And hasty it was, and Utopian, it was too
credulous of human nature, thus to identify offhand Christian rights with natural freedom, as if
democracy were but the civic side of Christianity,
or Christianity the religious side of democracy.
One is reminded of the error of the States General
in France in 1789 which, in their idealism, energy,
sincerity, and reasonableness, Acton calls ' the
most memorable of all political assemblies.'   But,
he says, ' their one error was that, having put the
nation in the place of the Crown, they invested it
with the same unlicenced power, raising no security,
and no remedy, against oppression from below,
assuming or believing that a government truly
representing the people could do no wrong—as
if no barriers were needed against the nation.'
Cromwell truly had the authority of the Gospel
behind his people.   Their rule was not unlicenced.
Where he and his were mistaken was as to the

extent to which the people at large practically
owned that authority. But if the attempt was
premature, and in much fatal, it did not kill the
idea. The institutional Commonwealth fell, but
its influence as a principle has been enduring
and commanding. It did open the way for the
emancipation of natural rights, of political freedom,
and of the personality of the State, from ecclesiastical and theological control. And it thus set up
the prior condition for Christianising them all
through, by the creation of a free Christian ethos
bound to take public effect in collective political
conduct.

The whole Calvinistic ethic was worldly in the
best sense as compared with the Lutheran. It
had a world-policy where Lutheranism had but
a bourgeoisie. And it was a Cromwell made, on
this side of him, by Calvinism that became, what
Gardiner calls him, the founder of England's
material and commercial development. He was
the translator of the best public ethic of the
Reformation, *i.e.* of the world, into modern history.
It was thus English Independency, and not the
aristocratic republicanism of Geneva, that made
Calvinism the formative power of the new world.
It was in the struggle of Independency that the
issue was settled between monarchy of the continental type and monarchy of the constitutional,

between old monarchy and the monarchy of the new world, as the form in which public right receives its best and safest scope. Amid the dissolution of the medieval order with its supernatural controls and securities, it has been a diffused, modified, but mighty Calvinism—a Puritanism far more than theological—that has supplied, however sub-con-sciously, the staying and ruling·power of the new order. It began in Holland, culminated in England, and expanded in America on a vast scale, which greatly affected even the French Revolution and every state in Europe. For an hour Cromwell succeeded, with an army which tried ' to set up a bran new fabric on ground levelled by revolution.' But an army even of saints (we have seen) cannot make a State, as soldiers do not make statesmen. Yet it closed one age, opened another, and made a future. It was the first and greatest attempt in history up to its date to incarnate a truly Christian idea of the State ; and it failed but as incarnations do fail—only the more widely to conquer. The idea was started on a career which could not be stayed. What was done could never be as if it had never been. And its motive power was radical religion —ethical and spiritual, individual and intimate ; and that meant radical politics—though all in an evolutionary and constitutional way in the long event. The autonomy of the religious community, we have seen, was bound to affect sympathetically the political community. Toleration arrived and was bound to pass into equality, and finally into justice to all churches by the complete detachment of Church and State as organised bodies. The political autonomy of the people is the inevitable, though not always the direct, result of this religion; and (leaving the question of what is meant by the people) it is the only line on which a truly Christian State is possible. And it was Independency, in spite of its miscarriage, that both showed and opened this way. The Reformation came there to its great and true public self; whose renunciation has been a blight on its Low Church champions that no pietism makes good. England served herself heir to the new moral discovery, by virtue of that appropriative and practical genius which makes her often slower than the idealogue nations, but more permanently effective for their ideas; which ideas would otherwise but beat their wings in vain, seeking entrance on political reality, as the venerable idea of a free people had done for two millenniums. Christian faith must always aim at a Christian State and Christian politics, even if the Church is not the lever, and not the loom, but only the power-house in their manufacture. The idea of a Christian State must always remain as real and powerful as it was in the Middle Ages.

L

Only it is a State made Christian, not by organic
connection with the Church, but by the moral
effect of the Church's gospel, working through
the personal faith of Christian citizens, and
massing that experience in a social tone and a
public policy.   If the Nonconformist conscience
is sometimes below its own ideal, the Independent conscience has been the mightiest of historic
powers in the modern world.   Democracy is safe
only as Christian democracy.   And the Christianity
of democracy is not according to its theological
belief (which is indeed a vast matter, but the concern of a church) but according to its personal
religion and its public conduct of affairs.

Calvinism (it has been seen) through its predestination doctrine, gave a valuable point of
attachment to Anabaptist spiritualism, but it
was not captured by it.   As the positive protestantism in our Independent genius, Calvinism
kept itself above Anabaptism in such matters
as positive belief, a cohesive church, an organised
state, and the right of war.   Independency did
pass ˙ through a Tolstoian stage in the early
ferment of the Commonwealth.   It is in a Tolstoian stage now in some respects.   If Quakerism
be defined (on the lines of Barclay's *Apology*) as
the last and purest form of the spiritualistic move-

ment, finely rationalist in its theology, and comparatively indifferent to the elements of dogma, of symbol, and of history in Christianity, cherishing a Christianity of practical piety in the form of enthusiastic spirituality and social sympathy, discarding sacraments and living by the inner light, then it might be said that Quakerism, if not growing in numbers, has so grown in influence as to have affected much of our Independency to-day. But Independency is not Tolstoian, it is not Quaker, it is not quietist, not illuminationist in its genius and history. In Tolstoism, whether as politics or doctrine, it dissolves, as it was dissolving when Cromwell saved it. It is much more than a refurbished Anabaptism, an unchartered spiritualism, a boundless subjectivity, a promiscuous liberty. Its religion is not spirituality but faith. And its polity is not sheer autonomy, which, unless it is the autonomy of a final, controlling, and social Gospel, always dies into atomism and anarchy. Such individualism is but an intrusion and repetition in religion of the political idea of personal right and independence—that helpless thing which a religion is there not to repeat, but to subdue, control, and fructify. The interest of Independency is not so much the autonomy of the Church, far less of the individual, but of the positive Word and Holy Spirit; nor is it the freedom of the

pulpit, but of the Gospel. Its enemy is not an
organised church, but a discrowned and deflated
gospel. To do no more than transfer natural
independence to the Christian religion is to bleed
the Church to death. It is to disintegrate it in a
narrow, fanatical, and remorseless veracity. And it
is to leave the soul to egoism, faith to subjectivism,
and the State to anarchy. Religion can afford to
be individual and autonomous within the Christian
pale, because there a positive Gospel has a social
subduing and regulative power on the soul singled
out for freedom. And it is thus essentially different
from the natural right to liberty, which has not in
itself the secret of its own control. The methods
of the one cannot be transferred to the other.
And the lesson of the Commonwealth's failure is
that we should keep them distinct, though not in-
sulated. The error of that great time is the error
of many still. For we are not enough influenced by
history; which we tend to regard as a museum and
not as a school, or as a field where we sowed the
wild oats of our past and not the seed of our
future. The Commonwealth failed by treating
England as a Christian nation in the same sense
as its church was a Christian church; and it tried
to regulate the unprepared people accordingly, by
direct and even forcible insistence on Christian
ethic. The natural Christianity which it repudi-

ated in its creed it postulated in its politics. And the event showed the effect to be as fatal in practice as the belief said it was false in theology. The Christian should be rigorist in his own personal ethic ; but a rigorism enforced on public practice is fatal, till the Cross of Christ is established in all hearts; then it forces itself. Human nature and society has a law of its own in the divine economy, with an evolutionary logic which cannot be arrested by any Christian barrage. It can only be turned by a long, slow, and gentle curve, engineered by a faith which has something more than an ideal eagerness, which has the practical sense and art of a situation.

This discovery represents the evolution undergone by Cromwell's own mind. The point came with him, as with Luther, when he had to break with the spiritualistic part of his supporters. The year 1653 was for the one what 1525 was for the other —the rupture with the ultra-radical and atomic elements, and the reaction to a certain conservatism bound up with a historic salvation, whether in belief or affairs, common to the first century and the sixteenth. By the same discipline Independency is learning to suspect direct political pressure, and to respect moral permeation. Sudden conversion is impossible with a modern State, which is no longer the clan and retinue that adopts the religion of its chief. And forced conversions are avenged in violent reactions and restorations. Enthusiasm must not in public matters despise opportunism. Idealism is impracticable, and can even be bloody, if it is so fanatic that it feels degraded by compromise and an instalment system. The kingdom of God still works by an elect and its radio-activity. The most encyclopedic idealism lives but in a little world and sect if it think to *force* its cosmic range upon the belief or practice of the great public. Even Christian discipline itself may become in this way a principle of anarchy, as, conversely, Christian liberty may destroy Christian truth. In the name of the Spirit men may cast loose from all revelation which controls either thought or life, all revelation outside their own visions, truths, or feelings. Revelation may go down, trodden under foot by a crowd of revelations out of hand. And then the field is open for any dictator, who will be pope or pagan according to circumstances.

It remains to be seen how far Independency can yet serve the great cause and idea it infused into the world. To-day we are all being forced out of our insulation into a vivid, and even organic, cosmopolitanism. The compression of the earth by the extensions of communication means a great expansion of the ecumenical, the humanitarian, idea, if we but rightly rise to it. Both the nation and the Church are being forced into the career and concert of Humanity. For the Church at least this means a call for a Humanitarian Gospel. But that does not necessarily mean a popular gospel, though it does mean a public. A puritan gospel of moral and intellectual thoroughness cannot be promptly popular. It does not mean a gospel of mere sympathy, but one which assures the moral destiny of Humanity on all the absolute security of God. And that again does not intend an ideal destiny for mankind to which destiny God is but the supreme means. Such a view would make God tributary to man. But it means a great *dénouement* of the Human Tragedy in the Divine Drama—a Gospel in which man with his tragedy and sin does more to glorify a saving God than with his achievement he does credit to a helping God. It means that we do not move from the Gospel which gave to Anabaptist liberty and subjectivity its only stability, and fixed its spirit in the Word. But it means also that we so re-read that gospel as to keep it still at the moral centre of the new world which it has done most to create. We have in places lost something of that gospel's faith and enthusiasm. We are tempted to seek a liberty which is independent of it, and even critical of it. But we should

be perfectly clear in our mind that such a liberty
is but a relapse into the short, atomic, and suicidal
Anabaptism which already we found so good a
servant but so ruinous a master. It is not our
first call to wait upon the liberties of a natural
democracy, but to descend on it, and to provide it
with a freedom which alone can secure these in
permanence and safety.

In one way the Toleration Act was a calamity to
Independency. It gave it only a right within the
State and not to the State. It excluded it from
all national office and responsibility. Worst of all
it shut it out from the universities and the universal
note. It gave it a freedom only to be smally free.
It helped to make it oppidan, conventicular,
seminarist. It drove it in upon itself, to cultivate
in religion a family piety, and in theology a provincial creed. Being compelled to be non-national
it became creedal. Secluded from the great national
issues it was thrown upon its traditional theology,
without the great inspiration of that theology's
origin, or the generous corrective of public affairs.
From this period date most of the elaborate
Calvinistic trust-deeds, which now give so much
trouble (where they are not neglected by consent),
because they seem to have been constructed
rather to stop holes against heresy than, like

every act of true worship, to make a great confession in face of the world.   The Anabaptist
element quite disappeared, both as energy of
spirit and freedom of thought.   In the matter
of belief the eighteenth century is not a time of
which Independency need be extravagantly proud.
It was devoted to orthodoxy, and orthodoxy
whose architecture was of a late, debased, and
perpendicular type.   Naturally it was Calvinistic,
but it was Calvinism with high sides rather than
high summits, Calvinism often with a lid on and
the air exhausted, the Calvinism of the lesser minds
and the lay pieties, Calvinism devoid of the grand
note it had in Calvin and Edwards.   It was Calvinism without the atmosphere of the great tradition
of Church and State, which gave an amplitude to
theology, and kept it close to history on the one
hand and to the Gospel experience on the other.
We are all familiar with the different utterance of
one of the greatest Independents and most thorough
Calvinists of the previous century, John Robinson.
He said in his final charge : ' The Lord hath yet
more light and truth to break forth from His Holy
Word.'   There is nothing startling in this to those
who know the spacious times of the great Reformers.
Calvin himself might have said it with his large
manner and his liberal exegesis.   It is quite impossible in reading the context to suppose that it

means no more than Dexter tries to make it mean—
changes and modifications in Church government.
It meant theology not polity. Robinson was
saying no more than many of the Independents
who avowed the Anabaptist influence had already
said when he went on: ' The Lutherans could
not be drawn to go beyond what Luther saw ;
for whatever part of God's will he had farther
imparted and revealed to Calvin—they will rather
die than embrace it. And so also the Calvinists—
they stick where he left them. A misery much
to be lamented. For though they were precious
shining lights in their times, yet God hath not
revealed His whole will unto them. And were
they now living they would be as ready and willing
to embrace farther light as that they had received.'
He then referred them to their Church covenant :
' Whereby we promise and covenant with God,
and one with another, to receive whatsoever light
and truth shall be made known to us from His
written Word.'

Dexter is much more valuable in research than
in interpretation. It is not easily intelligible how
words like these should be thought by anybody to
mean no more than modifications of Church polity.
But the most significant thing about these words
(which unfortunately we only have at second
hand) is the appeal from all theology and all

orthodoxy to the Word of Gospel, and the advice
constantly to verify the reference. '*Ad fontes.*'
Back to living sources and saving facts. We find
the note in all the great documents and occasions of the Reformation, in the Confessions, in
the Savoy Declaration, and even in the Solemn
League and Covenant, where the reference to
orthodox truth is quite subordinate to the reference to the Word. The eighteenth century
lost that reference out of its practical procedure,
however it may have held it in theory. And
the nineteenth showed the inevitable reaction and
even revolution. The stiff orthodoxy of the
eighteenth century was followed by the sentimental
heterodoxy of the nineteenth, and the critical
heresy of the twentieth. And it may be hoped that
in the twentieth also the pendulum will drop to
rest in the Eternal Centre, and we shall recover upon
a new base of positive faith and critical freedom,
well found in soul-stuff, brain-stuff, and food-stuff.
That base of course cannot be the Bible understood
as infallible, but the Bible as the shrine of the
Gospel. And our methods must be adjusted to
that great change. But the fountain of the free
Spirit must still be the Word of the Gospel breaking
into a thousand heavenly lights, yet working as
the positive act and power to change the race from
death to life.

Our reaction of the nineteenth century came partly by spiritual infection from the evangelical movement outside, and partly from the necessities of the mind itself, especially under the illumina-tionist influences of scientific thought. This re-action grew mightily under Coleridgean and Broad Church auspices. Mackennal says that Maurice had more effect on Congregationalism than on his own Church. It was at least a different influence. In his own church his influence has moved to High Churchism—he was always suspicious of the Broad. But with Independency it worked the other way. It made at first a generation not rationally but evangelically broad ; with a *Ver-mittelungstheologie* which represents a genial effort similar to the attempts to offer a Harmony of the . Gospels in the face of modern criticism. But that only prepared the way for a Broad Churchism which unhappily laid much less stress on the churchism than on the breadth, and followed continental criticism more closely than evan-gelical theology. It also fell under the close of the Romantic movement, and was far too much dependent on literary religion, as represented by names like Tennyson, Browning, MacDonald, and their various dilutions. Sympathy took the place of conviction. The passion for liberty of belief rose to a great height, partly at first

because Independency was so sure of its evangelical base. The old Anabaptist temper broke
out in this liberal direction with a force in some
cases extreme. It found its opportunity in the
state of theological education in the colleges of
forty or fifty years ago. And it attracted the
younger end of the lay mind in particular. It
threatened to become detached from a historic
Word and an evangelical Gospel in a practical
mysticism and philanthropic religiosity which was
more natural than supernatural, more sympathetic
than sure, and more rational than positive, keen
for effect and indifferent to truth. The ministry
on the whole was sound (though sometimes bewildered), because it is kept in closer contact
than the active young laymen with the soul's
deep need and guilt. Independency is indeed
a lay religion, and its ministry is in principle a
lay ministry. But in practice the ministry is set
apart by two things—by the necessity for handling
the Bible, and the duty of ministering it to the
actual soul whose confidences it receives. The
layman is in Christian contact with wrong and
reform rather than with sin and salvation. He
is a pragmatist. And he is apt to forget, in his
practical impatience and his instincts of immediacy, what the ministry has constantly to face
—that the conscience is more than life, the soul

more than the heart, holiness more than pity, and moral growth much slower than civilised progress. Till that is realised an impatience of theology is apt to drive the lay mind into sympathy with a spiritualism whose shining but shallow breadth is fatal at last to revelation, because negligent of the historic Word and the apostolic truth. Christianity is a lay religion. But it is so because it turns upon a universal priesthood rather than a simple sonship. The Fatherhood of God *sans phrase* is not Christianity, nor is the native sonship of man. We cannot have too much lay agency so long as it is the agent of a mediatorial religion and not simply of a kind fatherhood, of a redemptive and not simply a benignant grace. Our Independency is once more called on to do what Cromwell's did, and to shed the sectaries of an absolute rational independence, whose naïve ideal is an uncharted freedom with spiritual instincts, a sentimental or subjective religion with a theological Agnosticism. Independency can never give up its theological liberty. And creedal completeness, pure doctrine, is not its ambition. But it does feel, and it shows in this time of stress that it feels, what its history records—the necessity of founding its libertarian enthusiasm on a positive gospel, and securing its freedom on a revelation whose root is elsewhere than in the mobile soul of an individual, or an age. We can but end in wreck if we have more wind in our sails than ballast in our hold, more passion than pilotage, and more way upon us than steering power.

Allusion was made a little ago to our exclusion from the national universities, and to the inadequate training which, up till recently, was given in the colleges that so wonderfully rose to make that misfortune good. It was a deep and deadly policy that strove to neutralise the Toleration Act by cutting the root of the nerves which kept our mind alive. It was truly and malignantly thought that if we were prevented from having an educated ministry we should need no more toleration than the dead. To a considerable extent that policy was thwarted by the resource with which small academies sprang up round the more able and commanding ministers. The culture there given would be very inadequate now, but it was not far behind the culture of that age, and often commanded its respect. Then the enemy took the farther step of enacting that these seminaries should be closed—a provision which, for various reasons, never came to the effect it intended. But valuable as the work was which these schools of the prophets did, and marvellous as those colleges came to be which grew out of them by the generosity of far-seeing and spiritually minded laymen,[1] nothing could compen-

---

[1] Our present provision for training our ministry rests on a belief of our fathers in the higher education which does not exist so widely in our churches to-day. They contribute to it very little.

sate for the seclusion of the education of the chief
teachers of the public from the intellectual foun-
tains of the national life. It will be long before
the stamp of that misfortune on our treatment of
truth and affairs is lost.

But a new day dawned when, in 1836, London, as
the first of the new universities, opened a degree to
all without respect of creed ; as also when in 1871
the abolition of tests at the old universities admitted our youth, though not our ministry, to their
culture. But, valuable as these opportunities have
been, they have not been pure gain. Access to the
old universities has lost to us by attraction many
whom we should gladly have kept. And the effect
of London University on our ministry was at
the very first a mixed benefit. As there was no
divinity degree, and most of our postulants for the
ministry do not yet come to our colleges equipped
with the Arts degree, students were unhappily
allowed and encouraged to devote the whole or the
best of their college time to its acquisition. The
result was in some cases that they went out to their
charge with one or more good, and even brilliant,
degrees, and much knowledge in everything but the
matter of theology which it was their first business to
handle in their profession. They were unschooled in
theological method, and in the order of philosophy
which properly belongs to it (which has not ruled

at London University).   Added to this, the type of
theology offered by such prelections as they did
attend was not always of a commanding, or even
of a formative, kind in many cases.   It was of the
nature described by Dr. Dale in his somewhat con-
temptuous comparison of the Union's Declaration
of Faith in 1832 with the massive Savoy Declaration
(*Dale's Life*, Book VI. ch. iv.).   It was moderate
Calvinism, immoderately diluted, and set in a somewhat amateur philosophy.   The ablest students
therefore were well disciplined in secular regions
of minor value for their proper work, and less
well equipped to handle the real theological
problems of the hour.   Their intellectual respect
and even enthusiasm was sometimes preoccupied
by secular knowledge and rationalist methods, in
a way whose worst fruits we see in the results of
the same education in India.   And they imbibed
what in a few cases was a Philistine contempt for
the rational value of their own religion in comparison with its sentimental side.   Some were
tempted to bestow the training they had on a
criticism of their faith's traditional form, instead
of an exploration of its mighty content.   They
were sometimes graduates in useless science and
amateurs in necessary theology.   They respected
Mill, loved Tennyson, and trounced Calvin.   Some
few had to pick up as they could, during the

M

first years of their ministry, when the mind's first plasticity had been pre-engaged for other methods, such theology as they acquired; and then sometimes it was by mere reading rather than study, which left them much at the mercy of current, and even weekly, literature. When it is remembered also that the chief concern of their life was preaching, and preaching of a kind that must attract the public; farther that their relation to their people might be based on mutual sympathy rather than a common salvation; it will be realised that their views sometimes grew up in an atmosphere of impressionism, which left them still more at the mercy of the Zeitgeist, when they should have been provided with a culture that commands it, and that can come from a deep and ample Christian theology alone, with a belief of fulness and not simply of point.

But within the last generation a great change has taken place, and one that will mean very much for the future both of the ministry and the Church. More than twenty years ago Springhill College, Birmingham, became Mansfield College, Oxford, under the one powerful teacher among us whose theology had the cosmopolitan note. And then in 1900 London University was converted from a mere examining body to be a teaching body also. A theological faculty was also set up, which was composed, as to a moiety, from the theological schools of London Nonconformity. And, above all, a degree was instituted in theology. The example of London was followed by Manchester University, and will doubtless be followed by the other new universities wherever they are in the midst of theological colleges numerous enough to form a group of schools and a faculty. The student for the ministry can now therefore have the university stamp and training in the very subject with which his life has to do. The courses are adjusted accordingly. Both the teaching and the study are obliged to rise to university standard. Our colleges never were so staffed and so efficient as they have now become. They have never had such a competent and cosmopolitan note in their subject. Their teachers are among the first in the land. The student has himself to blame if he pass into the chaos of the age without a chart or compass. And there is hope that Christian truth will return into the stewardship of men as competent, and even massive, in their grasp of it as those giants were who made us, and who were as great apostles as they were powerful theologians. In the matter of faithfulness and devotion ready to be duly guided, we were never more rich than to-day. And amid all the confusion and stridency of the time it is much that Independency should be still as evangelical in its note as it strives to be adequate in its creed.

But in this connection it is not to be denied that we have difficulties in our own household. The colleges of Independency should be its pride. They alone enable the churches to meet the first claim on a church—the adequate preaching of the Word to a world. And no church has more reason to be proud of what its elect members have done in the way of making good our exclusion from the national universities. But I say its elect members, not the Independent churches as such. The colleges are private trusts, of which Independency has the unspeakable and gratuitous benefit. They were founded and endowed by private men or groups, not by the churches, and they are not controlled by organised Independency, which has all the benefit and none of the burden. The churches are in the unsatisfactory position of receiving their trained ministry as a charity. The subscriptions from churches are insignificant, the interest is small, though the provision and maintenance of a ministry is the Church's very first charge. The Independent churches, speaking generally, are not sufficiently alive to either their treasure or their duty in the colleges. And though the Congregational Union, led by the ministers, legislates more and more for a ministry duly trained, there are symptoms surviving of that indifference to a professional culture which alarmed Cromwell and his friends. Such culture forms what might be called the reserve power of the ministry and its ' second wind.' There are those who would be content that the ministry should pass through no more than a Bible Institute, if only it can preach in the sense of immediate impression on crowds. Some seem even to look for more from the preacher than from his Word. It is an outbreak of the old Anabaptist spirit detached from the Reformation Word, or fallen into a pleasant pietism.

The Anabaptist strain in our double origin is in several ways very persistent in our history. Its subjectivism tends to sacrifice evangelical religion to temperamental or rational. I have indicated how it has broken out on the rational side as a protest against theological certainty, and for a truth which is but what every man troweth. I have hinted, farther, how on the enthusiastic side it broke out, through a somewhat crusted soil, in sympathy with the great evangelical movement, and with the Broad Church movement on its evangelical side. I have spoken of its enthusiastic readiness to consider and absorb the spiritualistic movements of the age. And we have the same trait

emerging in the indifference of some of our people
to a trained ministry for the future, if only the
preacher is momentarily or subjectively effective in
the present. They tend to think that a sound training damps the spirit, as Christian ethic chilled the
negro camp-meeting. They are apt to forget that
the Church is itself the great preacher, and to sink to
providing a mere pulpit, or even a springboard, for
the preacher. The Church is in danger of being
exploited by the preacher rather than served. In
the small churches this is a serious difficulty, as
they are apt to fall a prey to illiterate but fervid
speakers, whom they invite to their oversight, and
thus foist into the stated ministry. Against this
risk the Congregational Union has had to legislate.
And even the larger churches sometimes are less
apt to be impressed by what is competently said
than by how it is agreeably said. They are apt
to respond to piety rather than to faith, to the
interesting rather than the strong, to the magnetic
rather than the apostolic. Effectual calling is lost in
effective. It is the hour of immediacy, mobility, and
impressionism. The immediate, the edifying note of
the mystic prophet for groups is apt to be more
welcome than the regenerative note of the positive
apostle for the world. The Church may be sacrificed
to the audience. What prospers a congregation
may be more regarded than what makes and builds

up a church.   What interests monied men for its
activities may mean more to it than what writes
souls in the book of life.   All this is a phase of
the spiritualistic note detached from the apostolic
Word, or the effective severed from the evangelical.
The passion of spiritualistic Humanitarianism tends
to displace the inspiration of the Holy Ghost, the
power of the Incarnation, and the act of redemption.   Some would even find in such consecrated words as these only the debris of dead
theology ; and, if their ministers needed any
training at all beyond an Arts degree, they would
rather have them taught economics, sociology,
pedagogy, literature, and, perhaps, first aid.
Only the extreme people, of course, would put
their wishes in such terms, but it is no exaggeration to say that the evangelical type which
holds the hour is the simple, soothing, winsome,
and helpful, rather than the convincing, convict-
ing, converting, and creative.   And the order of
speech most welcome is that of the gracious
hierophant rather than that of the searching seer ;
the speech of sorrow, sympathy, healing, rapt
hope, and spiritual beauty, rather than of sin,
righteousness, judgment, saving faith, and God's
supreme glory.   It is the Catholic note of the
beatific vision rather than the evangelical note
of the kingdom of God.   Its note is æsthetic

rather than ethic, the beauty of holiness rather than the power of grace.

If the ministry craved for is so temperamental rather than evangelical, this, I am urging, is a phase of our old Anabaptism ; it is against that adequate training of the ministry which tells most powerfully when the flush of young ardour has subsided ; tells as a reserve, and makes a man a rock and not a reed. For to reach the region where the Gospel's creative and staying power resides means much labour, patience, and pain, as well as vigour and joy ; but to utter one's own spiritual personality need not cost much—till the Nemesis arrive for coining the soul to the public instead of rightly dividing the word of truth.

Yet the feminist weakness I speak of, and the danger (for it is no more), is only part of the price we must pay for the much-needed humanising of faith. What our truth loses in the greatness of Puritan imagination it gains, to an extent at least, in sympathetic contact. We get nearer men, even if we do not always come to them from nearer God. The Gospel sits down beside them, and brings a cheer which was often lacking to the mightier truth. Of the two extremes who would not prefer that of nineteenth-century sympathy and alertness to eighteenth-century orthodoxy ? The disciples, who loved Christ

and failed Him, were yet nearer Him than correct
Judaism.   And they became apostles, which even
genial Judaism never did.   Religion, indeed, is not
Christ's just because it is genial.   There was little
genial about either Him or his greatest adjutant.
But geniality is the under surface of a holy love
which promises more than the harsh veracity of
critic or cynic.   Christianity is not indeed the
religion of the heart but of the conscience, and
humanising means moralising; but the Christian
way to the conscience lies oftener through the loving
heart than the able head.   And all the acuteness
of the mind does not penetrate and subdue the soul
like the subtlety of the spirit which believes and
therefore loves.   The point is that the love which
stays and which tells is not our natural sympathies
turned on divine things, but the fruit of a supernatural change in which the heart is remade by the
Spirit through faith in the Word.   The natural affections are not made Christian by being turned on
Christ, as art is not made religious by painting saints.
What we have to do with is the gracious affections,
which spring up when Christ is turned upon us,
turned with a searching and saving power from
whose piercing light nothing is hid.   That love does
not grow in a night; it is not temperamental; it is
the product of much experience of life, much study
of the Word, much spiritual severity, much toil

of sacrifice, much despair of self, much repentance under grace, much incense beaten small and
cast on the consuming fire, much silence beneath
the peace of God. ' That thou mayest remember,
and be confounded, and never open thy mouth any
more, because of thy shame, when I am pacified
toward thee for all thou hast done, saith the Lord
God.' To be silenced thus, to dwell on our salvation till it silence us thus, is a first condition of
sacred eloquence, and death to sacred rhetoric.
It is a frame that is not cultivated by fluent and
facile religion. But it makes stammering lips and
struggling thought more sacramental than gliding
streams. His voice is as the sound of many waters
—which do not sound except they fall and break.

The political ardours and the theological extravagances sometimes associated with the Anabaptist
side of Independency are efforts on its part, tentative
and empirical but dimly conscious of its own right
way, to replace itself in the great world-stream of
action and belief, to emerge from the orthodox conventiclism into which it was partly forced and partly
fell, and to reintegrate itself into the great Church,
the great democracy, and the world's thought. It
is an instinct quite inevitable in any church that
knows it has a world-gospel, and knows the world
that needs it. No great rediscovery of the Gospel

has ever aimed at a mere repristination of its grasp by a previous age. Luther, for instance, did not just tumble into his contemporary world with a vehement iteration of New Testament themes. He condensed in his own person the moral problems special to that age and to the generations before it ; he did not simply throw a gospel in their face in a Low Church way. Because that was not how his gospel struck him. It did not smite him in the face, it got to his actual moral case, pricked and converted him in his heart, him as he actually was, him as generations made him, him the medieval man with the age's quest raging in his soul. The Gospel acted on him experimentally, and this was the badge and seed of the new time. The old answer was fitted to the new problem psychologically. It was adjusted to the conditions created for the conscience by all the generations that had developed the Church's unrest around him. The questions that Luther answered with his gospel were not first century questions any more than twentieth. They were medieval questions. And the Reformation answered them by a gospel and a principle adjusted to them with such intimate and telling knowledge that in the long run it dissolved medievalism without surrendering its own specific power for the future.

It is the like thing we must do to-day. We

cannot answer the questions of a monistic and immanential age like our own with the medieval idea of God—a God to whose transcendency the world was optional or accidental, and one of several equally possible.   We cannot answer questions about revelation in the same way as was done by our Independent fathers to whom the Bible was identical with the Word of God.   But the answer is still and always to be made by the same Gospel as the apostles preached as the intimate power of God for redemption.   From that foundation Independency can never depart.   Its history has had, and can have, no other ground for its firm, flexible, and permanent freedom.   No idealism has the secret of permanence as a freedom.   Like all culture it sweeps round to dictation and dogmatism, to sets and cliques.   Freedom is the product of a gospel and not of a culture.   We have to repeat Luther's method, in another plane and climate, but with the same Gospel.   It is claptrap to glorify the heroism of our fathers if we have lost their source of courage, and their power to fit positive and permanent Christianity to the new time.   Heroics without such power are but the stage *bravura* of futility. And yet our fitness for the time is not, any more than Luther's, to be measured by the extent to which we can present social panaceas, avert or quell the wars of hard taskmasters and infuriated

peasants, or provide Utopias for Mr. Bernard Shaw.
How shall man be just with God ?   When the wage
question is settled there will still remain that question of sin's wage, which the Church's Gospel came
chiefly to take in hand, and to recast society from a
new centre.   That is where the Church has its positive, creative note.   Beyond all our protests against
abuses and anachronisms it is there, in the conscience,
that we have to justify our existence, and speak
the divine Word.   Let us take steps to be sure of
ourselves there.   Which means that we win a new
certainty and depth in our gospel ; so that we are
sure, not with the iron certainty of a truth which
has rusted into its place, nor the wooden idolatry
of a God wooden too, but with the vital power of
a creative principle.   To give Independency new
confidence in itself and its genius, to restore power
to its pulpit and conviction to its pews, to cast off
its present soft apparel and put on the armour of
God, we must care less for liberty and more for that
which makes and keeps it.   Independency must
remember, first, that it means a real Church of the
Holy Spirit ; second, that it is built on the one
foundation of the Church and source of the Spirit—
repentance toward God and faith in Jesus Christ
as sole Lord and Saviour ; third, that its internal
freedom both in thought and act is secured to it as a
church by that redemptive, creative foundation alone;

fourth, that its first social service is due therefore to the great apostolic Church of the Spirit, and especially to the uniting of all the churches, with a relative independence, on the one evangelical spiritual base; and, fifth, that it must exercise the true Church's effect on public affairs for the sake of the kingdom of God. It is impossible that Independency should ever lose a commanding interest in public affairs. It would be a misfortune, and a fatal one, if it did. And its genius lies in political affairs rather than social. Only let us not think that our public value is to be measured by our popular favour. And let politics in their party form be kept from entering and exploiting the churches as churches, engrossing their interest, and prescribing their methods. It is churchmen that should be politicians and not churches. In this respect the churches have to avoid the fatal extremes of the Commonwealth on the one hand and the eighteenth century on the other, and to breed Christian politicians without becoming political institutions like an Established Church. Let us beware of the political establishment of a disestablished Church.

LECTURE VIII

HAVE we not arrived at a time when the question whether Congregationalism is worth preserving, or has a future, must be placed on a new basis ?

Our fathers were brought up in an age when it was held that Independency was the true polity because it was the polity of the New Testament Church. But we have discovered (or it has been discovered for us) that the state of things in the New Testament, while it was neither Episcopacy nor Presbytery, was something very different from our Independency. And even had it not been different, we now take a different attitude to it. We think the polity then is not necessarily the polity now, that what was inevitable for church life in the first century need not be equally valuable for the twentieth, that no polity has divine right, that several are equally useful according to circumstances, and therefore equally divine.

But when that has been admitted, upon the word ' useful' the farther question rises at once, useful for what ? And the reply has been forthcoming with much enthusiasm—useful for human liberty, or equality, or fraternity, for the ideas and purposes of democracy. Congregationalism was declared to be in the nature of a democracy, and so to be democracy's congenial form of church. And the democratic idea included the liberty and development of the individual, together with the growth and progress of the community and ultimately of humanity. Christianity was the enthusiasm of humanity endowed with a divine charter. And no doubt this was a great and needful stage in the onward upward march. But not only have we become somewhat disillusioned about the individualist democracy, as Mr. Hobhouse's book shows, not only are we somewhat concerned about its claim to entire autonomy, and not only are we less sure about the kind of humanity which forms the democracy's enthusiastic ideal ; we ask another question. Passing by the doubt whether a church gathered about a King can be a real democracy, we ask whether the Gospel is there for the uses of the democracy or the democracy for the uses of the Gospel, whether it invites mankind to exploit God or to glorify Him. We observe that *the democracy will recognise no authority but what it creates, the Church none but what creates it*; and the collision is sharp. We ask whether the tribunes of democracy really mean that we should transfer to

it the claim made for itself by the Roman Church—
that it not only serves the kingdom of God but that
it is that kingdom, and is therefore the grand rival
of Rome for the reversion of history. It occurs to
many to question if democratic liberty, fraternity,
and equality are the be-all and end-all of moral
humanity ; to ask where place is left in that list of
rights for duty, and especially for man's first duty
of obedience with heart and soul and strength and
mind. They note that the higher, and finer, the
more original and pioneer the issue, the more likely
mere majorities are to be wrong ; that Christ gave no
sign that He came to set up a final and millennial
state of democratic liberty ; that He was chiefly
concerned with something which had an eternal
right to rule and use liberty of every kind ; and
that if political liberty could ever be finally shown
to be incompatible with His ideal, purpose, and
action, then political liberty must go down, like
every other natural instinct or ambition similarly
incompatible. It is remembered also that it was in
no idea of political democracy or individualism that
Congregationalism took its historic rise, but in an
obedience to Jesus Christ in the face of all the
powers or majorities around it. It was the mother
of political democracy and freedom, but not its child.

A modification of the democratic plea for our

N

existence is put forward when it is said that we
exist for ' social service.' I have suggested that
our tradition and genius are more political than
social. But in so far as it is true that we exist for
that social end, it is equally true for the Church in
all forms; and it is not easy to see what ground it
gives for our separate existence, especially consider-
ing the advantages in this direction possessed by
more highly organised bodies with more immediate
prestige. The movement for social service by the
Church of our time is one of the greatest. It corresponds to the evangelical movement of one hundred
years ago, of which indeed it is largely a fruit. But
if it is put forward as *the* ground for the existence
of any church, or its title to public respect, it still
seems to make the Church valuable chiefly for its
service to the kingdom of man rather than God.
And the note of many Christian people who are
engrossed with this idea is the treatment of Christ as
its greatest asset rather than its Lord and God, its
most powerful force rather than its Life and King.
Truly, the Gospel is social or nothing. It came as
the salvation *of a historic world.* The grand unit it
confronts is a world. It at once created a Church,
which is its first social charge. Its first charge
is its own society, the new society which it is its
nature directly and inevitably to create—the Church.
The service of man is but its second charge, through

the first.   The first social work of the Gospel is to
make and cherish its own society of the worshipping
Church, and to keep that first ; and then to serve and
bless man with all the collective resource that such a
society alone has because it is full to overflowing with
faith, and love, and power.   It does not look well when
that social service seems to be prudently adopted
by the Church (like the newly discovered right of
the parent in education) rather than inspired and
irresistible.   It would be a false position, and the
source of much futility in our effort and influence
on society, if ever social service were prominently
associated with indifference to Church or belief, if
it were even treated as a substitute for evangelical
solidarity, as an anodyne for an inner spiritual
void, or a means to cover or recover a lapsed
faith.   The Church is something more than a co-
operative society dealing in social welfare.   Yet
nowhere else is the secret of social welfare.   Far
be it from me to disparage, or to reduce by one,
the philanthropic or social services of the Church
to general society.   The Church is not doing too
much for society, if it were doing the right things.
It is not doing nearly what it could.   But one
chief reason is that it has in many cases become
more concerned about the society it would serve
than the society it is ; more concerned about
man's welfare than about God's condition of it,

and His provision for it, and especially His social provision of a Church made by a real gospel in which the journals have no interest. The Gospel must do more than it now does to socialise our churches after the inward man before they can do God's social service to the world. There must be more spiritual, more evangelical solidarity. We are not doing what we should for society because we are not turning out in sufficient numbers people whose first social ardour is for their church and its trust from God. We are not for society what we should be because the Church is not the society it should be; and Christian men are not compelled and equipped in it to act on society as such citizens should, as churchly citizens alone can. The extensive action of the Church suffers chiefly from over neglect of the intensive. This is as true for its home effect as for its foreign missions. The great social action of the Church is not to bring pressure to bear on the State *quâ* Church; but, by becoming the great home and nursery of the only social inspiration that really masters egoism, it has to produce such Christian citizens as must and will combine to apply the direct pressure required. The Church has a far greater action to exert on society than its ministers can have. It touches and moulds many things which its pulpits should not. Whenever direct pressure has to be applied we

enter party politics; and the great variety of
opinion on party and other lines breaks up the
volume of solidarity in the Church; where something more valuable for reform than even reform
itself is generated, where the social soul is created,
the social unity rallied, the social inspiration fed.
And such direct pressure is therefore better applied
by leagues formed for the purpose, whose first and
express object it should be, than by the standing society of the Church, which has for its first
charge the moral and spiritual solidarity of faith.
Spiritual solidarity means more in the end for
social effect, social reform and progress, than does
any social programme.   And a church saturated
with spiritual love of the *brethren* in a common
faith is the true focus or hearth of that love of
the *neighbour* which is the moral condition of
social eugenic.

Dislodged therefore from its final ground in the
New Testament practice and in social utility,
Congregationalism is driven back to ask what
distinctive ground remains to it. It has done a
great work, one of the greatest of historic works—
it has given birth to modern democracy. Is that
not enough for one sect to have done? Might it
not consider that it should retire from the stage,
like Israel when it had produced Christianity?

What has it done since ? To that question there is a twofold answer. It inaugurated modern missions (especially in its Baptist branch), and it was the backbone of municipal and local public life. But allowing for these things the inquiry persists. What is it equipped to do in a modern world ? For what does it still exist ? Why should it be cherished still by modern-minded men who realise the problems both of the present and the future and yet believe ? Why should it be served and believed in by the best men and the strongest ? What does it confess in a distinctive way ? To what does it give effect ?

To religious liberty, it will promptly be said by many. Now I have already indicated what was meant by religious liberty among the sons of the Reformation. Its prime sense with Luther and all his train was not freedom among men but freedom before God. It was not freedom to hold any religion or none, but the freedom which was religious or nothing, the freedom which was identical with Christianity, freedom not of action or opinion but of soul. Forgive me if I repeat anything in trying to be explicit on a point so great.

There is a religious liberty which is the child of our Independency, and there is one which is its parent. There is our freedom among men for God begotten by our freedom in God for men. In a like

way when we speak of political freedom we may
mean one or both of two things. We may mean
freedom in the State from an individual, or freedom
from the State for an individual. We may mean
the freedom of all the citizens from a ruler who is
despotic, however benevolent ; so that each man
has his responsible place and right in the ordered
State as a whole. Or we may mean freedom for
each individual from the interference even of a free
and republican State in the region of his thought,
conscience, or faith. It is this latter—the laicity
of the State—that is the great product of the
Reformation; and it goes on to disestablish the
Church everywhere. It goes on to secure the
State's ecclesiastical neutrality, and to place the
establishment of Christianity in the ethicising of
its politics alone, and the production of a Christian ethos as the national spirit. All this was
utterly foreign to medievalism, which knew but of
the *imperium,* or universal State, at the absolute
service of the Church. It is quite true that the
Reformation in its empirical beginnings had this
inherited note. And it has not, in England as
elsewhere, succeeded in surmounting it entirely by
its intrinsic principle. There are many remnants
of the theocratic idea still lingering in such venerable places as the coronation service. It took
English Nonconformity to give to the Reforma-

tion its true self, and realise in practice what it really meant by religious liberty.

The Reformation did not propose as an end religious liberty in the political sense. It was not a battle for liberty but for truth. It did not, and does not, care for liberty except as a product of the truth and for its sake. Truth is the Church's aim, liberty only the means thereto. And the truth which concerned the Reformation was not the truth of the intelligence or the reason but of the soul, of salvation. It was saving truth and not scientific. It was the truth as it is in religion, and not in the schools. The Reformation asked (I have already said), What is truth—salvation by the Church, or directly by God? And it answered—salvation directly by God alone. This carried tremendous public consequences, which history was to unfold, and chiefly by Independency. But these consequences were not the conscious issue of the Reformation, which dealt with their Gospel cause or postulate, and not with themselves —as the way of the Church must always be. When Luther spoke of Christian freedom he had no idea of the rights of man or of classes. He and his friends did not in the least mean each man's liberty within the State to choose his own form of worship. He meant nothing so modern, so proleptic. That is liberty of conscience, and what preoccupied the

Reformers was something higher and more fundamental—liberty of soul, religious liberty in the
ultimate sense of the word.   In the modern use
religious liberty means the liberty of each citizen,
as such, to be free even from God, to be an Atheist
without loss of rights.   But in the strict Christian
sense religious liberty means freedom before God,
in God, ' no condemnation,' freedom of intercourse
with God, unhampered by guilt and the demands
of a law which God has now made His own charge
and become responsible for in Christ.   It is the sonship of faith, the being at home, not in society, but
in the Father's house and kingdom.

There was another conception of religious liberty,
which we have seen arose alongside of the Reformation though not from the same root, and which
came into violent collision with it—the liberty
claimed by the peasant movement and the Anabaptists.   For these, in part, liberty meant freedom
from the tyranny of the feudal lord, and in part it
was a soul freedom based on an appeal to the newly
opened Bible ; and it insisted on the reorganisation
of society offhand according to the Sermon on the
Mount.   It demanded a radical reform of society
apart from the deeper radicality of Luther's new creation by grace.   It was urged by plain and pious men,
who took the Bible as a code and charter of public
right, and found it to counsel the subversion of all

force and government. Freedom from the State was the ideal, not freedom in it. They were the Tolstoians (I have said) or pacific anarchists of their day, though pacific they could not remain. In a crude way they anticipated many of the ideas of religious liberty which only a later age realised. And they had a great and early influence upon the form of Independency (as has been shown), though they did not furnish its inspiration or its anchor. These came from a deeper source, by way of Geneva, and they were rooted and grounded on the Word rather than on the Spirit without the Word or above it.

It was the intimate liberty which *is* religion, and does not simply flow from it, that established Independency; it was a liberty conferred, not won; which in turn produced civil liberty. Spiritual release produced 'religious liberty.' And for us this must always be the case. We do not stand simply for civil liberty, but for civil liberty on a spiritual and evangelical base; not for a free State, but for a free State as the product of a free Church of men whom Christ has set free. That is the genius of our existence. We must always live *on* our cause, though we live *for* our product—on free grace for a free State. Our secret is in our inward and spiritual freedom, not in our outward and public. And the power in that secret, the power which as a historical fact produced civil liberty, was nothing else than the gospel of justifying and regenerating grace in Jesus Christ our Lord and God. It can never be anything else at last. Nothing else exists which gives the guilty conscience experimental and practical freedom with God, and so makes him his own freeman with men. And what has been here said about civil liberty applies to theological also. It is a secondary, though inevitable, product. It is not our reason for existence.

To take this last matter at another angle. In the extreme demand for theological liberty there is something that is not clear to me on the one hand and something that surprises me on the other.

It is not clear to me that the claimants are always sure about what they mean. In connection with religion liberty may mean freedom of knowledge or freedom of power; freedom to reach truth or freedom to declare it. It may mean freedom of research and thought or freedom of Gospel and speech; freedom to pursue truth not yet attained, or freedom (in soul or circumstance) to publish truth revealed once for all; freedom of theologising or freedom of prophesying. Which have the claimants chiefly in view? Freedom of research, in theology or elsewhere, belongs to the idea of a university, which must

refuse to be bound by the past or by any finality.
That is the freedom of the schools. And it is a
very great matter, for which men have worthily
fought, suffered, and died. But the freedom of
prophesying, of publishing truth already ours,
whether won or given—truth not now pursued but
regarded as final in respect of progress and crucial
in respect of destiny—that belongs to the idea
of a church; whether it be the freedom wrought
in the soul by such a Gospel compelling us to
its utterance, or the freedom allowed by society
securing us in its utterance. The university is
organised in the interest of the one freedom, and
the Church is, or should be, organised in the
interests of the other. And their reciprocal service
should not destroy their distinctive genius.

Now it is not clear to me which liberty is the
leading concern with those who demand in our
churches a freedom absolutely unchartered. As
churches we have always supposed that we were
created and organised in the interest of a final
Gospel and its publication, a Gospel of historic
revelation and not of future discovery; that is to
say, in the interest of a religion given, decisive,
personal, and practical. We are not organised in
the interest of a theology, that is, in the scientific
interest of developing truth, but in the interest
of religion, that is, in the evangelical interest of

realising it and spreading it, the interest of giving away what we already have by gift, and not of reaching by effort what we have not.

And this is where my surprise awakes. The demand for the extremest liberty in our churches is made in the interest of a progressive theology. That is to say, it is desired that they should be organised for theology as tentative, for theological research and experiment, that they should be so organised as to promote the culture of all sorts of views on such subjects, out of which ferment theological progress may emerge by the survival of the fittest. That is to say, really, the Church is to be organised as a university (and a bad one) and not as a church. There is the confusion. And the surprise is that the demand is made by people who are always telling us that in a church the great, ruling, and forming thing is religion and not theology, and that the theological interest is very secondary, and, when it gets the upper hand, mostly mischievous and obscurantist. Why then should a church be reorganised in any such interest, in the interest of a liberal theology, of a comprehension latitudinarian instead of positive? And if it be said that it is not claimed that the Church should be organised in that interest but in the interest of religion pure and simple, the only answer is that there is no such thing possible, and

that their keen interest in the rationalising of it
shows this. It shows the keenest interest in religious
content, the renovation of religious content. Religion is meaningless or non-existent without an
object, a revelation with statable features. And
as the object or revelation is so will the religion
be. And the statement of that object and of our
relation to it is some kind of theology. And the
only choice is between one theology and another,
between the theology revealed as the principle of
the final Gospel and some more subjective theology
which is either incompatible with it as heresy, or
destructive of it as paganism. And as the Church
was made entirely by a positive final Christian
gospel it cannot possibly be organised in the interest,
or on the principle, of a religion which is but in the
making, which is neither Christian, final, nor positive as yet, but is only free and inquisitive thought
in an atmosphere of religiosity.

But the plea that Congregationalism exists to be
an arena for unqualified theological liberty, and a
cave of all the religious winds, is hardly worth dis-
cussing, as it does not seem to be put forward by
any who are familiar with the genius of a gospel, the
nature of a church, or the history of our churches.
Unqualified religious liberty is but love in a mist, and
it ends in the convictions of ghosts, the energy of

eccentrics, the anarchy of egoists. It is going behind
a long history and victory, which it ignores and
wastes, in order to start a new spiritual struggle for
existence from the very foundation, and to make a
ring for a conflict of warring religious possibilities,
out of which the Gospel may emerge or may not.
Liberty can only exist as qualified. Everything
turns therefore on what qualifies the liberty. And
there again everything must depend on what creates
the liberty. For in all spiritual freedom its only
final authority is its source. Its normal principle
is in its origin. And the source of Christian
liberty is not any natural right—certainly it is
not so in a religion of Redemption. Christianity
is not a divine charter for natural independence—
for the recalcitrant, the turbulent, the *condottieri*,
who make no churches, but only troops that dissolve with them. It was born, as its servant,
Independency, was born, in something that created
a new liberty, and did that only by first creating a
new and greater obedience. It put in our hands a
new and greater trust than our freedom, something
which made us free and able not only to serve but
to serve *it*.

The question of our right and call to exist takes,
therefore, a new form at the present hour, though
its answer still means a return to the New Testa-

ment where our fathers founded us—only it is a return to the *Word* and not to the *Book*. What is asked of us is what is asked of every church which does not set up a monopoly of exclusive foundation and divine right. Are you, with your methods and organisations, well calculated to serve in a distinctive way the Gospel that God has given, and to secure its authority? Is Congregationalism, worked as it is for practical purposes by the majority principle, able to keep the trust, and put out to interest the capital, of a Gospel which creates and maintains a church as the supreme agent on earth of the kingdom of Heaven? Is such a Congregationalism able to guard and exercise this one trust given by God to men for the realisation of the New Humanity; especially when the Word is unpopular, and disappoints the people rather than wins them? Can its majorities be trusted to keep the faith, the word, and the power once for all committed to the faithful, and to keep it whether it succeed or not? Majorities may be naturally religious; they are not naturally Christian. Can a church which must, by its structure, be largely exercised in obtaining majorities for its necessary occasions and decisions, have the real presence and guidance of the Spirit which in history has mostly mocked majorities and worked by martyrdoms? To such question we answer, yes.

We are Congregationalist with good ground and hope
that we do on the whole have that Holy Spirit
and that living Word which make the real authority
over authoritative majorities, and preserve them
from the spiritual suicide to which they naturally
tend. We take many risks. Faith always does.
Liberty always does. They can easily be abused
and travestied. But we believe that Congregationalism is worth keeping, and worth sacrifice; though
only for its possession and service of that which
makes a church a church and for its facilities in
applying it to the public situation. We possess
at the base of our being a living Christ, a positive
Word, and a Holy Spirit, which alone have the
right and power to control the majority principle,
and to subdue it to be a principle of Church action
in democratic times and conditions. We represent
that principle as safe and good for spiritual purposes
only when the community is composed of people
whose souls are made by a positive gospel, and to
whom it is more dear and effectual than any
successes—even its own. That is to say, Congregationalism is workable and valuable when its
ruling power is its chief treasure—not the majority,
not mere truth, but the Word final in the Spirit;
which Word, and not mere religion, we have to show
flexible enough for modern conditions; but which
Word also must be all the more positive with us

o

because we in particular, with our loose organisation and our lack of a creedal standard, have nothing else to protect us from majorities whose vote and freedom might land us anywhere on a passing gale.

Congregationalism would never have come into existence if each church had not believed itself to possess in an infallible Book, opened by an infallible Spirit dwelling in the Church, sufficient authority to protect it from the gusty vote of the hour. The infallible book is gone, but none the less are we compelled, if we are to be permanent churches and not passing clubs, to replace it by some authority with equal power and right to rule decisions as they fall to be made. If we are without such an authority in our midst we are not churches, and we have no future; we have no right to boast of the old Independency as our past, and we have no right to look forward to a Christian future. If our decisions as churches are simply taken as the verdict of natural common-sense applied to religious issues, like the vote of any local authority, town council, or parliament; if we do not really believe in the present guiding Holy Spirit of a living Word and Gospel in our midst—then we are not churches; and we are bound to lose, to communions that remain real churches, those members who take the church idea in most earnest. The infallible book has gone, but the infallible and historic Gospel in it has not gone, nor, as we believe, its infallible and present Spirit. We have a Gospel historic, positive, decisive, and final, and we have the living action among us of the Spirit Who put it there. There lies our standard and control. We have an infallible Guide; and, if not always an infallible apprehension of His guidance, we have a growing apprehension of it, and always a faith in it; our faith has an infallible if our intellect has not; so that we may make mistakes but we are not wrong, and we are cast down but not forsaken, and we lose engagements but are on the side that has already won the campaign.

But if the whole book be plastic to criticism, and if our experience of the Spirit be explained away by the new psychology, if we but take stand on anything so subjective as the Christian consciousness of the day, then since that consciousness has no organ such as Rome, we are driven to mere consensus. But consensus is practically majority. And Satan cannot cast out Satan, nor the majority principle be its own authority. A real authority therefore is even more needful to our loose-hung liberty than it may seem to be for churches more organised. And if only we have it our course is safe and clear.

I have pointed out with some fulness the great part played in our origin by a spiritualistic Anabaptism whose tendency was to override and ignore the creative, normative Word. I have spoken of the footing this movement had in the doctrine of predestination. And I have said that it became valuable to us only by being prevented from becoming master, and by being kept in its proper place. This we were able to do in virtue of three things :—

First, by the fact that the predestination was a predestination *in Christ, i.e.* in Christ crucified and risen, in the Word of His Gospel. Even with predestination the Spirit was not independent of the historic authority of the Word.

Second, by the rallying and controlling power of the Bible Word habitually used as the source of the Spirit, and not simply its correlate.

Third, by the English genius for local self-government and the larger politics, which gave us, in political liberalism and democracy, an ordered outlet for the individualism that dissolved the religious communities when it ran riot there. That genius has not left us, if only we show ourselves able to effect the transfer which must be made under the second head, if we can replace the Bible by the Gospel as the lynchpin of our liberty, and carry that Gospel clearly in our soul and openly on our forehead.

We have much heroism among us in the moral

courage of men who are willing to face for their views a lifetime in great minority, unpopularity, and ineffectiveness—some of this heroism we have even running to waste. But what we have to rely on most is the greater spiritual courage to make the grand evangelical committal—to commit the soul and the world, amid all the seductions, bullyings, distractions, or criticisms, of the hour, to the final and ageless Word of the New Testament salvation. There is but one note of the true Church ; and it is not subjective but objective, not our mood to God but God's charge to us ; not a subjective spirit, like charity, but an objective relation, like faith. It is the note of the Gospel of the grace of God to guilty man in the Redeemer. We have the Church, not where we have the mere temper of Christ, but where we have the Word of His reconciliation, and that Word in actual experience, and authority, and effect by the Holy Spirit. It is a temper only because it is first a power, and a power through those in whom it is more than a sweetness. For did gentle Melanchthon not truly say, *Summi adversarii nostri sunt suaves theologi ?*

Our personal concern in the great historic act of God's salvation must be *at least* as intimate, passionate, and practical as our interest in commerce, criticism, home, civics, or politics—if we

keep things in their New Testament perspective.
It certainly is so in the New Testament. The
Gospel is at least as personal and close an interest
as home, country, or business, and for the most
part much more so. And as long as we keep that
book where we do, and yet invert in practice its
standard of value, there must be inner friction and
weakness. Many churches do observe that order
of importance, many individuals. But it would be
well to realise that no church is really a church or
really free unless that be the perspective, unless
that is recognised as the principle or ideal, however far we tarry behind it on a given stage in
the evolution of our practice and the degree of
our approach. And the real issue between the
Free Churches and the rest is deep beneath the
controversies that heat us ; it comes to turn more
and more on the place we assign in our practical
interest and affection to the Church of the Gospel
in the life of the Spirit. High Church says, ' I
believe in the Church more than in the State.'
Broad Church says, ' I believe in the State more
than the Church.' But events have shown that
Broad Church has no stability. It disappears
upwards into High Church, or downwards into no
church. And so it must be with the Free Churches
that are more interested in the State than in the
Church, and allow the mental habit of the Gospel

to be quite subdued to the mentality of the State. A vivid interest in citizenship is no new thing among us. Two generations ago our great laymen everywhere made the mainstay of municipal and political life in their locality. All we feel to-day but develops this immense interest and influence exerted upon public affairs, and especially municipal affairs, by our fathers, and especially our grandfathers, in the formative years of democratic freedom and civic life. To surrender that interest would be to surrender their principles ; we are not true to these principles unless we develop that interest. But the principles were in their case applications of a very positive faith and personal piety. And we should not be true to them if ever we became more interested and more intelligent in citizenship than in sanctity, if ever as a church (I do not speak of individuals) we are more concerned with sorrows than sins, with wrongs than guilt. We should then have to choose between a disappearance as churches into religious clubs and associations, and a firmer grasp of the High Church idea upon which alone a Free Church can rest. Congregationalism at least is High Church or nothing. It began with men who were ready to do anything with the State that the Church might be free and autonomous, men who held that the last word in history and affairs was with the true Church, and not with any amalgam

of world and Church ; which usually meant that
the world secularised the Church more than the
Church spiritualised the world.

In proportion as the Church is divided up,
i.e. as stress is laid on the local and congregational
element in it rather than the universal, so much the
more stress must be laid on the common faith, if
the idea of a church, its unity, and its right to the
comity of other churches, are to be cherished at all.
The local association must be balanced by the
common confession, tacit or explicit. We have
never stood for absolute and unchartered liberty.
Those who did sought it elsewhere. It was men
agreed about the substance of the New Testament
Gospel that made all the claims in our past for
liberty, and guarded it so jealously. It was done
in the interest of a great, free, and apostolic Gospel
and its development ; it was not in the interest of
a general and genial religion. They had no other
source of their liberty than the Gospel, and no
other worthy object of their sacrifice. The whole
issue is raised again from the beginning, and
from far beyond the beginning, when the right
is claimed to deny and discard the apostolic
Gospel. There is no right then to appeal to
our traditional liberty, which has been entirely
a freedom *within* the apostolic Gospel and not

from it. And the great Church could not be
expected to co-operate with a church where
liberty went so far that everything was an open
question if only we cultivated the spirit of tolerance and charity, or even a love of Christ.
That is not Christianity but Tolstoism. It is
not Christian charity but genial Judaism. The
point is that in a church whatever is relaxed
in the way of organisation must be more than
made good by concentration on a real experienced
and confessed Gospel of Word and Spirit, and not
on Spirit alone. And accordingly Congregationalism can only hope to survive, and it is only
worth preservation, enthusiasm, or sacrifice, according as its liberty is both fed and balanced
by a very powerful gospel, whose theological
progress and social service grow out of positive,
personal, and immutable belief on the eternal
things that matter for the soul and its salvation
in Christ. No liberty is worth a church's while,
no sacrifice even, which is bought at the price
of all taste for worshipful reflection on God's
eternal work for spiritual destiny, which makes a
people grave, wise, and tender in its creation of
the future from the past.

The great question before us, therefore, is not
connected with our work or our machinery for the
Christianising of society, but with God's. And it is

the question whether we can prove in practice that an aggregate of small and separate churches is equal to a charge so great and integral as the first trust God has committed to the Church for the world—the trusteeship of His only means for Christianising society and effecting His kingdom—His historic, apostolic, final, universal, and eternal Gospel.

LECTURE IX

FOR a church what it believes is of more moment
than what it does. Its belief is the thing that
created it, and it is the constant factor which
makes the continuity in its varying action. It
inspires the action which is but fashioned by
the hour. The Church is founded on faith, else
it has no foundation at all; and on faith not as
a subjective frame, but as our collective relation
to a given object of holy Love, an object which
gives itself in grace, and in that act creates the
faith. Were faith chiefly a subjective frame there
could of course be no statement of it. A mere spirit
hath not flesh and bones. You cannot define an emo-
tion; you certainly do not spread it in that way.
But, faith being an objective and living relation,
some living statement of it is not only possible
but necessary if it is to be conveyed to others or
confessed at all. We may say therefore, without the
intellectualism which too often detaches belief from
faith, that Christian faith always carries implicit
in it a Christian belief, without which we can tell

219

it to nobody. And the Church's first duty is to confess in some form this common faith which gave it being. But if that be an act of worship (as all true confession really is) it can only mean the confession of the object and matter of faith. It does not mean an exposition of faith. And it cannot mean the profession of the Church's subjective attitude. The Church says but ' hear me ' ; it does not say ' look at me.' For then the Church would be preaching itself ; and we preach not ourselves, nor our experience, nor our faith, but Christ crucified. We preach Christ crucified not in our martyr experience but in a historic and final Act, which creates the experience that takes it home, and does not simply hallow an experience it finds. The prime duty of the Church is not to impress, nor even to save, men, but to confess the Saviour, to confess in various forms the God, the Christ, the Cross that does save. The Church is there as the great confessor, in thought, word, and deed, of its Creator ; and its action, varying with each occasion, is only a special form or corollary of its central confession that it owes itself, its worship, and its world to the glory of the grace that saves. The Church's activity in the world and for it is but one phase (which might be called the lateral phase) of the Church's perpetually ascending

worship. *Augustius a latiori differt.* It works not
simply because it believes but chiefly because of
what it believes. Its belief is more than its work,
for it creates it.

That is so in regard to the Church. For this or
that individual it may be in a measure otherwise.
His work may be more valuable than his belief;
first, because his work is a part of the work of a
believing Church which devised it; and, second,
because there are many other individuals to represent and preserve that true proportion of faith
and work which he may have lost. So that the
individual may with far less peril than a church
put action before belief. But if the Church make
this error the mischief will not appear in the span
of an individual life, but it tells fatally on the
generations to come, and in a range proportioned
to the truth concerned and to the greatness of a
church's power for good or ill.

But we have run to an extreme individualism
even in the Church. In dissolving the difference
between priest and layman we have levelled down
instead of levelling up. We have reduced the
priests to lay 'lack-wings' more than we have
lifted the laymen to a royal priesthood. The lay
idea is uppermost in both our ministry and our
laity; and the lay mind, especially in religion, is

individualist, and is apt to hold even its social theories in an individualist way. Our ministers are laymen more than our laymen are ministers. And what we need is that the ministerial element should be uppermost in both our laity and our ministry. I mean this. Ministry is Christian service and self-sacrifice, and, if there be a contrast, laity is Christian self-assertion; and the Church's ideal would be that lay self-assertion should only be there in the ministerial name and spirit of self-sacrifice. The Christian can only assert himself as a *social* unit, one of a body, not of a crowd. But to that we have not yet come; and we are apt to treat personal faith as if it were but individual religion. The individual also, speaking generally, is still concerned more for his freedom than for his sacrifice. His first point of honour is, not that he shall sacrifice and obey, but that he shall be free to sacrifice or not as he will. And Congregationalism is more welcomed in many quarters because it offers a protestant and unchartered liberty than because it gives facility for obedience and service in the Holy Spirit. We have run to individualism in our ideas even of church life. Because for an individual a belief may matter less than conduct does, we jump to the conclusion that the same is the case with a church. And this individualist stamp we have transferred from the relation of church members to each other, and we have printed it on our churches as communities. We have let it settle their relation as churches to each other. Of churches also it has been thought and said, as if they were but magnified individuals, that what they do, or how they feel, is of more moment than what they believe. The 'spirit of Christ,' by a like subjectivism, is made of more account than the faith of Christ, or than the Holy Ghost.

We fall therefore into two classes—though they are of very unequal size and weight.

1. There are some who claim that Congregationalism permits no limit of belief either tacit or explicit, unwritten or written; that it is a mere creedless polity or 'apolity,' conceived in the interests of absolute freedom and sympathetic relation in the region of religion; that it is entrusted with no charge having an unbreakable entail from a historic revelation; that our freedom, therefore, is the one thing that we have to assert and guard, in order that truths with which we have not started may emerge as supreme from a perfectly free trade in opinions, and an unhampered struggle for existence between beliefs. By a generosity which has more geniality than justice, this amorphous liberty is defended by some mild

idealists who do not need its benefit for themselves. It is held, in fact, that as Congregationalism is but a polity it is not essentially different from Unitarianism; nay, it has even been claimed that it contains nothing to exclude from our pulpits the denial that Jesus Christ ever had a historic existence.

2. The second and far predominant class consists of those who say that Congregationalism came into existence only on the basis of historic, apostolic, and evangelical belief; which to abolish is to alter fundamentally its constitution, and not only make it another church but destroy it as a church altogether. For Christianity is evangelical at its centre or else it is another religion. But (they say) within the pale and by the power of such an evangelical faith there is room and need for a great development of theology. For which development a large range of freedom is necessary. And the due freedom is best secured by a belief which though positive is unwritten. This view, I say, is the dominant one in Congregationalism. And it has served well on the whole, but only on the whole. It has left some belief very nebulous, and made nebulosity too tolerable. What remains to be seen is whether it will carry us through the totally new conditions of the future as it has so far carried us through the past. For now the whole

situation is altered by the fact that the great
issues are not so much those of formal theology,
but of the historic facts and spiritual powers which
make any theology possible. They are not theological variants but two religions, not a religious
difference but a different religion.

As to a creed it has never been denied by Congregationalism that it has a creed ; the only question
is how it holds it. And we should distinguish
several questions in this connection. We should
first ask, Must a church have a belief ? And to
that we can only answer that so long as it remains
a church it must. The Church did not create its
belief, it was created by it and not by a vague
religious impulse ; therefore it cannot discard it
and remain a church. We have then to ask whether
that creed must be specified, formal, and written,
be it long or short. To which the answer is that
in most churches it is so, but not always. The
question, where it is not so, is answered by Congregationalism. *La tradition c'est moi.* It has a
creed but it is not a written one. Like the pope
it embodies its tradition of belief. Its creedal
cohesion has rested on an honourable, tacit, and
evangelical understanding. And a written creed
it is not likely to have, either until events show
that the unwritten understanding is unable to

P

secure the apostolic Gospel, or until the other
churches, before entering on closer relations of union
and co-operation, think fit to adopt a common
expression of their basis, message, and purpose to
offer the world.

Our future has a new feature which was not in
the past, and it corresponds in a striking way to the
political situation of the hour. It is this, that the
constitution itself is being referred to the popular
vote. What a constitution is to a State that a
belief is to a Church. And, whereas up to now it
has been a question of particular measures or
doctrines to be accepted under a constitution, the
question now, both in State and Church, is as to
the *locus standi* of any constitution against the
popular vote. Could a vote of the public abolish
king and lords ? Should mass meetings of work-
men repudiate the leadership of their organised
representatives ? Could a vote of the Church
abolish its constitutive belief ? The questions are
all *au pair*. They are but different phases of a
great social movement, which might become a land-
slide. The Church is different from the State,
however, in this respect, in that the one possesses
in its creedal constitution a final gospel, deposit, or
trust which the other does not ; and it is therefore
above the utilitarian considerations which for the

other must be chief. There is nothing in history that the State could not amend or annul in the great interest of the nation ; but that is not so with the Church. No consideration of utility could justify the abolition of its historic gospel. But so far the analogy holds, that the constitution, or the question whether there should be a constitution, has now come down from the lawyers or theologians to the lay arena, and is bandied in the streets of the city and the lanes of its press.

The pointed form which the question takes in the hot politics of the hour is, first, whether the public will in a vote is the will of the nation, and, second, whether that vote should be taken, on the old representative principle, by an election of responsibles, or on the new mass principle of a plebiscite. The Conservative party has surprised many by moving for the latter. Which has been explained by some as the extension of an old policy to weaken the dignity, responsibility, and power of the Commons, and to carry forward the new principle which Lord Beaconsfield imposed on the party in a former crisis, of directly coupling up the monarch and the multitude.

But be that as it may in regard to the State, what concerns us and our form of the Church is this.

For us also the belief which is the constitutive element in every church is on its trial—and not even before a jury, far less a judge, but before our public. All that we have as a constitution is going to decision ; and it is going where we have always had to take other and minor questions (however great)—to the popular vote. On this vote, however, up to now the constitution has always had a guiding and controlling effect. What will the popular vote do in the absence of a constitution, *i.e.* when it has to vote not *by* an accepted constitution of belief but *upon* it ? For of course when we vote upon a constitution we do not really vote by it, we only vote whether we shall vote by it. And we vote by referendum.

For with our churches the mode of voting is settled. Our churches have not representative government. They are not Presbyterian. They have not a legislative eldership but an executive diaconate. They are pure democracies, and they act by referendum. In theory everything should come to the church meeting. The deacons' court is not really a court, it is a mere committee or executive ; and nothing it does is valid till a church meeting empower or endorse it. It is convenient often, of course, to ignore this principle in practice, but principle it is. We work by plebiscite.

And so far it has done well enough on the whole. But so far there have been submitted to it only the ordinary measures in the course of legislation, so to say. What is presented for this mass decision now is the ultimate question of Christian faith and the Church's existence. The constitution is coming to be the question, in a far deeper sense than Congregationalism discussed a few years ago when it changed its organisation. All that was but regulative ; the present matter is constitutive for the Church. And it comes to the membership as to the final court. The appeal is to a Christian adult suffrage. The constitution goes to the referendum, and is at the mercy of a sheer majority. This is a situation we have never yet had to face, and we are somewhat bewildered in facing it. Just as our English police system is not organised for dealing with armed anarchists, as it is too generously organised for a departure so new and destructive, so with our Congregational machinery. It has never had to contemplate and handle within its own community a challenge to the existence of the Christian faith. For the eighteenth-century Arianism was child's play to modern negation.

Now a plebiscite is all very well with a political question, where the principle of the matter is mainly utilitarian, and where the majority, if it give a sifted and considered verdict, has the power of the constitution in its hands by right. But it is a different question with the Gospel and the Church, where no possible majority, however long and severely sifted, has the right to undo or dispose of the final gift of God. He and His Gospel must be true in the Church they created, if every man be a liar. So that while on many grave theological points there could and should be accommodation, toleration, and a kind of co-operation, as of the two opposing parties in one legislative House, on this question in the Church there could be none, and heresy would be bound to end in schism between those who held to a final apostolic Gospel and those who renounced it.

But let us suppose this reference were made. Let us betake ourselves to the region of the political analogy, and suppose that the old Gospel, as constitutive of the Church, were submitted to referendum in all the churches.

It is agreed among constitutionalists that the referendum is, and should be, applied, not about a vague principle, but only about a definite measure, when it has been well discussed and formulated. But that clearly means, farther, that it shall be put into written shape. Both the *Times*, for the referendum, and Sir Frederick Pollock, against it, agreed upon that. If the constitution go to referendum it must be a written constitution. With the shunting of representative government disappears the glory, safety, and flexibility of our British politics—the unwritten constitution, honourably worked.

But what does that mean for us ? Our common and creative belief, unwritten so far, has been our constitution, the axiomatic base on which a majority system worked, and the final governor of its action. It is what we chiefly have had to protect us from the gusty majorities to which democracies with their idolatry of the hour or the orator are so liable. For its sake the Church exists as a spiritual nation, and its occasions majorities serve but do not command. If it give way we are a Church no more, and there is no longer a living body with either a minority or a majority. That belief is the principle of our action. And the mode of our action is the referendum. But, as I say, it is of the nature of a referendum that it cannot be worked without a written and definite reference, just as in Parliament there must be a definite Bill. The only constitution that can be submitted to our plebiscite is a written one. What then becomes of the unwritten creed when, as the constitutive belief of the Church (were it but condensed in one article), it must be submitted to the mass verdict ? Will an unwritten creed serve us when we come to vote on the Gospel ? Are we clear and unanimous what the Gospel is ? In the past even the unwritten base and bond has given shelter, facility, and plausibility to some movements for its denial. But if the creative creed became the great question of the future, could it remain unwritten when the issue arrived at the popular vote where all our questions come at last ?

I raise the question. I do not table an answer. But if ever this became a practical question there is one thing that should be remembered. The crystallising is a question of expediency and not of principle. On the whole, and at present, we may be better without such a document. But there is nothing in Congregationalism which makes a confession of the kind fatal to it. That could only be if we totally changed the Congregational idea, and reduced it to mean a first concern for unlimited freedom of thought, instead of a first concern for the Gospel which makes freedom, in the only sense in which freedom concerns a church—freedom of soul. If we are dealing with the Gospel as something *in* which we are free, and not with it as something *from* which we should be free, there is no reason why, in given circumstances, we should refuse to say to neighbour churches or to an inquiring world what our collective Gospel is ; and there might be very good reasons why we should say it for the Gospel's sake, whatever became of our Congregationalism.

This suggests other points of great moment. Declaration does not mean subscription. A declaratory expression by a community need not be a subscribed expression by individuals. The confession of a unitary church does not involve uniformity in every member, so long as it is not openly challenged, renounced, or defied. It is but characteristic and not coercive.

Again, a confession of faith is one thing, an exposition of faith is another. The confession need involve no more than one genetic article. It is not a theology but a statement of the Gospel. True it cannot be without developing a theology; for no Christianity can. But it is not itself scientific or explicated theology. It is a prime theology and not a secondary; it is more final revelation than tentative theology; more dogma than doctrine.

Yet, again, a great church on the dogmatic base of a prime theology must always tend to present a great world with a rich and ample theology. It must always move to declare its gospel not in a nucleus only but also in a plerophory, not in an essence but a totality, not by way of peeling down the onion to a portable core, but by way of rearing the germ to a spread tree. But in that case the confession, as it becomes expository, must

change its form when circumstances have ripened
to require it. All religion must have a theology
more or less detailed. It must have a doctrine
more or less explicit, unless it is a matter of
atomic sentiment. And the doctrine or theology
of individuals needs to become collective and ample
belief, if it is cultivated in the consciousness of a
community, if it express the mentality of that
community, and become the badge and burthen
of a church to a cultured world. The prejudice
against this amplitude of belief is strong among us
for reasons connected with our history rather than
with our principle. And it is encouraged by two
errors. One is that such theology must be final in
its form, which is Roman and not Protestant at all.
And the other is that it must be in the nature of a
decree instead of a confession, a statute instead of
a product, a standard instead of a register. We
ought to be at a stage of religious culture far
beyond such notions. When we really are, we
shall be free to discuss the expediency at any
given time of what our principle (so much richer
than we know) gives us full liberty to do. The
great thing is to recognise that it is equally open
to us so to act or not so (else we are not free). If
ever such a thing were done it would be entirely
within our principle and competency. But also,
and only, if it were recognised that any such public

expression of the general or average belief, while it
was standard for the time in the sense of being a
living church's corporate confession, could never
be so in the sense of being final and irrevis-
able in its statement, nor in the sense of being
imposed on each individual ; that is, it could be
used in no exclusory sense, but only in a declaratory and characteristic.   It could not therefore be
an end in itself but only a means, dictated by
special circumstances, toward the great end for
which a church exists ;   which is the confession
upon due call, whether tacit or explicit, of the
New Testament Gospel as the spiritual interpretation of the world, the secret of its moral destiny,
and the changeless authority that alone gives freedom its charter, its scope, its safety, and its service.
It is simply a question whether, in given circumstances, the free Gospel would be better served by
a church defining its belief in it or by not defining
it.   In either case the subsequent assent is left to
the individual honour of those who share the
Church's object and feeling in serving it.

As to the conditions which might force such a
step.   Already, on one side, on the practical side,
Congregationalism without a working constitution
more or less organised had broken down into a
sand-heap, and the old, granular, atomic Indepen-

dency is dead.   It had failed at its lower end, in
the poor and rural parts, where the extinction of
the yeomen and the drift to the towns had made it
in many places financially impossible.   It had also
failed in respect of the ministry; and the recent
regulation of entrance to the office was to exclude
the incompetent, or the otherwise dubious, who
trade on the ignorance and inexperience of un-
guided churches.   So that, by way of self-preser-
vation, Congregationalism has had in these matters
to adopt a written and express constitution which
would have seemed to Independents of sixty years
ago (who were very suspicious of the establishment of a Union altogether) a monstrous and
treasonable thing.   They believed, indeed, in conference, and not in absolute isolation.   ' We are
Independents,' says a document of 1645, ' no
otherwise than to distinguish us from the Episco-
palians and the Presbyterians ; for no true church
is independent.'   But it was in conferences *ad hoc*
that they believed, for discussion merely, and not
in a standing organisation.

But if Congregationalism began to wither at the
top instead of thus crumbling at the ground; if
a wave passed over it, like the Arianism of the
eighteenth century, which swept away into Socinianism some considerable scholars, pulpits, and
trusts of the body; if such a thing happened, if a

group of men arose with learning, piety, and moral
weight, and without ambition or eccentricity, to
promote aggressively the view for instance that
the Gospel was simple and non-mediatorial Fatherhood, that Jesus was no more the living Christ
now than Buddha, or that the Holy Ghost was
but a phase of spiritual force—then it would be a
difficult thing for other churches to co-operate with
us. Church union or federation would be thrown
back by so far. We might be left stranded in
negation. And it might then be felt that a time
had come to adopt something as clearly constitutive
for our faith as the union scheme of a few years ago
is for our works. But it would have to be something
in the interests of the free Gospel and not of a
correct orthodoxy, something more dynamic than
detailed, and therefore more in the interests of a
positive and permanent liberty than such a document as now stands in the Year Book, something
more like the declaration of 1878 (whose absence from
the Year Book is so inexplicable while the other is
there). It can be no interest of ours to synchronise
the clocks of thought, if only the Church and the
world are sure that we have the common sun.

There can be no public or social religion without doctrine. We cannot preach without it. We
cannot convey our personal faith to others without

it. And if that be so, it is necessary and latent in
that personal faith; which dies if it is shut up in
the close room of our own soul, because it gets no
chance of exercising its mind. The time is well
ripe for a reaction against the reaction against
doctrine, and in some of the best quarters it is
well begun. Theology was once a tyrant, but we
have turned it into an exile, while we idolised
eloquence or literature; and a restoration is over-
due. It must come back; but it must return to a
constitutional and not a despotic place. We have
been much too free in giving it up to the negative
and revolutionary critics. We have let ourselves
go too far for a church's health when we entirely
replace it by personal experience; as if we could
ever personally experience that salvation of the
whole world which we must both believe and preach.
That is an essential element of our faith, but it can
be so only as a certainty revealed theologically from
One in Whom it is already a conclusive experience.
We have gone so far as to say that if we cherish
the Christian charity we may part with Christian
doctrine indefinitely. We do not need (it is said)
any doctrine of the cross if only we own the spell
of Christ's inner life and sun our souls in His
inner light. But how impossible it is psychologically. Our intelligence is not one of three
watertight compartments which make up a float-

ing soul, and enable it still to float if one of them is destroyed. The man cannot be separated from his understanding, any more than from his feelings, or his will. It is the man understanding, as it is the man feeling or willing. And will, or feeling either, is bound to deteriorate if cut off from knowledge. Faith without understanding is as hollow as faith without works. Religion without doctrine is as vain as religion without action. The curse comes home on the one route as surely as on the other. Without doctrine religion is obscurantist; and an undogmatic Christianity is often the refuge of amiable indolence and comfortable lack of knowledge. You cannot progress, you cannot adjust your faith to the mentality of any age, if you refuse to give it intelligible form, and state it as truth. Revelation is not statement, but it must be capable of statement.

And if we talk of experience, how are we to rouse the deepest experience in others but by the doctrine which interprets the unique and final victory of Christ? The ultimate Christian fact is that whole New Testament Word; it is not a certain putative historic person, distilled by criticism out of swollen records, who believed so and so, but might have been wrong, or wrongly reported. It is not the fact of Jesus but the meaning of Jesus. Everything turns, not on the fact of a historic Christ (which alone is mere prophetism), but upon a certain interpretation of that fact, which makes up the New Testament, which is possible only as doctrine, and as a doctrine which makes Him more of a living contemporary to-day than if we were alive in His part of the first century. It is impossible to gather and keep any church round Jesus as a mere residual historic character, acting on us impressionally and not intelligibly. That is to treat Him as a deep, mysterious, and imposing figure, but not as a sure, final, and creative revelation. It is His interpretation as a final revelation that makes the Church—His interpretation as the clear light of God and not the dim depth of man, the very presence of God and not the apotheosis of the soul. It is on faith in revelation that the Church rests, and not on reverence for a mystery —even were that mystery the inscrutable Jesus, or the imposing Christ. He is what He is for the Church's faith, and not for its reverence. It is a bad symptom when a church has more to say about reverence or charity than faith, and measures by the one instead of the other. It is mere æsthetic. And for our faith Christ is Revealer and Redeemer. His position and action are theological; and theology is valuable as the only adequate confession *by an experient church* of what He is.

It is in such a theology that the Church's charter lies. These apostolic truths are its constitutional foundation against any number of votes, or any keenness of wits. The Church's life is bound up with the Church's doctrine. And a non-doctrinal church cannot but be a weak church, always growing weaker, till it go under to the democracy, or be squeezed out by true churches with this staying power. Revised doctrine by all means; but a Christianity indifferent to doctrine is a Christianity without Christ, and left by the Spirit.

If we consider the whole situation of the Church in the world, and especially its belief, we find it in a crisis comparable only to that through which it went in its collision with Gnosticism in the second and third centuries—a far deeper crisis than the Reformation was. It is not only surrounded by pagan influences of a somewhat refined and sympathetic kind, but it is invaded by them; and many do not know where to take their stand—on the core of the Word or the best of the World. Many indeed do not distinguish them. How then, we ask, did Christianity come out of its peril at the time I name? It was by concentration and consolidation into the Catholic Church. The Church organised her life and her belief from a positive and distinctive centre of faith in a

Q

historic redemption. It was so then ; must it not
be so now ?

But *mutatis mutandis.*

Then it was by a unitary organisation corresponding to the integrity of the Roman Empire. Now
there is no such thing as one Empire, either to
set the type or define the antagonism. We are
faced by a multitude of independent nationalities
and realms, which co-exist by concert and not by
coercion. And if the Church concentrate to-day
it can only be as the concert of many great independent churches. It can only be by the free
federation of their variety.

Again, in the early centuries the Church crystallised round a definite confession of its belief. And
federation to-day is no otherwise possible with
any prospect of permanence, whether the belief
is written (to work under the idea of right) or
tacit (to work under the idea of honour). Without publicly owning some common and positive
belief no church can continue to live or to act
on the world, and no churches can cohere. Un-
sectarian, undenominational, undogmatic Christianity is not Christianity at all. Federation and
confession therefore go hand in hand.

But in the early Church the union was effected
under an exclusory creed imposed on individual
faith, and always tending to define and to enlarge

itself, not merely as theology but as a final creed. This was inevitable under the mentality of that age. But it is just as impossible under the conditions and liberties of the present. In so far as the Church has a statement necessary for cohesive life and action it must be what I have defined as a confession of the Gospel rather than what has now the procrustean associations of an expository creed. It must be declaratory and not exclusive, the expression of a corporate faith, and not presented for the subscription of individuals. Its purpose must not be to eject heretics, but to tell the world plainly what our corporate message of its destiny is, to prevent the public from thinking that our truth is but what every man thinks, and the Church a concourse of atoms ; to afford guidance to its own young, and especially to the neophytes of its ministry ; and to enable heretics to define their own position by it, and defend their due freedom within it. It must be central and not peripheral in its truth ; and it must also be general and not particular in that truth, just as it cannot be particular to individuals. But it must be general by intense compression and not by vague diffusion, with a simplicity strong and pregnant, not weak and poor, comprehensive of power rather than of people, aiming at influence rather than area. It must be a gospel rather than a theology, the broad message of a preaching church, and not the specification of an academic society. In contrast, therefore, with the tendency of the creeds, it must be brief and not diffuse, synthetic and not analytic, by preference consisting of one composite article, like 2 Cor. v. 19 f. It must of course be, as to its form, always in the power and control of the living Church, and revisable from time to time accordingly. But the more brief, central, and evangelical it is, and the less analytic, scientific, and detailed, so much less will be the need for revision, and the more infrequent the occasion.

But we should first clear our minds on the point whether the deeply longed and prayed for union of the churches is possible without some such understanding. Then we can work as we pray. When we are sure about that, one way or the other, we can then either drop the matter, or go on to settle what form the consensus should take. It may be pointed out that where union among the evangelical churches is going most rapidly forward, in Canada, in South Africa, or in Australia, the creedless churches have either to stand out, with the prospect of being rubbed out, or they have to come in after securing due modifications in the way of liberal statement, and the constant interpretation of it by the living Church.

The great matter is that for leverage on the world without, and for liberty to our people within, to our young ministers especially,[1] there should be no doubt what our message and gospel is ; and that its confession may take any form, written or unwritten, best calculated in a church truly free to that end. There is a freedom from creed and a freedom by creed, and it is an old controversy which is the more free. But in a living church such a controversy could not exist.

What is the Gospel ? What do we mean by the thing we call salvation ? By the power of the Holy Ghost ? What do we mean by the Gospel and its Word ? How do we arrive at our true relation to Christ and to God ? Is it by the consummation of man's natural excellence, or by redemption from his natural perdition ? Is it by natural causes working historically, spiritually, and evolutionally, or by a supernatural, superhistoric power creating us anew ? Many who deserve our respect, in this and other lands, seem to think there is nothing in a pure Christianity that the former hypothesis would not meet, and thus the latter would become needless theology. They not only honour Christ but they

---

[1] It should not be in the power of any chance critic to accuse a preacher of betraying the faith without some centre of reference by which the accused may protect both his freedom and his honour.

feel Him.   Nor only so, but they strive to enter His
soul, and some even to immerse themselves in Him.
His spirit means for them His spiritual atmosphere,
his inner habit, which they desire to breathe.   He
is distant, obscure, and needs effort; but they are
willing, they are fascinated, to bestow it.   It is so
with the admirers of many a genius.   Take the
analogy of Browning.   He too is obscure, but full,
and even teeming.   What is his message ? what does
he mean ?   Many have pored, and still pore, on his
works.   And for their help they join a society of
others, gathered about the same centre, with the
same desire to master the master.   They privately
ponder the documents; and that they may do it to
richer purpose they form themselves into a fellowship of the like-minded.   They own the spell of a
mystery throbbing with revelation for such as are
the wrestlers, and not the strollers, of the soul.
And there is the piquant paradox of the contrast between his deep thinking in verse and his
ordinary appearance and talk in society.   So it is
with Christ.   There are many of the finer sort who
cannot and would not evade His spell.   And the
more He eludes them the more He elicits and
provokes.   They devote themselves to the gospels,
humbly, quietly, without any apostolate or any
attack upon others.   From these gospels they win
a view and even an impression of Christ, which

they extend and deepen by the aid of the fellowship, vitality, and tradition of the Church, or such
sections of it as they find congenial ; sections perhaps more inquiring than sure, more expectant
than convinced, more gracious than powerful, more
interesting than commanding, but still owning
the social, spiritual, Christlike note. Under such
influences they willingly call themselves disciples.
And they even confess Christ as their ideal, their
guide, perhaps their comfort. It seems so simple,
fresh, and spiritual. And no few in these days are
surprised that we should ask for more from any
Christian. ' That is good enough for me.' We are
familiar with this excellent side of the individualist type of reasonable piety. But individualist it
is, however pious and attractive. These people
wonder and regret that we do not stop where they
do—over the mystery of Christ's imposing personality. Why did not Christ ?

The great question is not what produces fine types
of individual religion but it is something else. And
something twofold. We have to pass beyond that
to ask, first, Does that valuable result after all do
full justice to the Christian revelation, the whole
Christ as given in the New Testament, even in the
gospels ? And, next, is it a result that can carry
a church, and so a world ? Surely, no. We cannot
read even the gospels without finding on Christ's lips

quite as much about Judgment as about Fatherhood, about judgment as an element essential to
a holy fatherhood; and does the admirable type
of religion I have named do justice to that? Nor
can we take Christian history as a whole, beginning
with the New Testament, without seeing that this
type could not carry the Church (however it may
be carried by it), and yet that the Church is
essential to the Gospel and Kingdom in the world.

What is lacking then in the type I have
described? Often, in the first place, insight or
patience for any plane of things above and beyond
its own young naïve realism, innocent of all the problems with which Kant and his peers floated out the
new age. And, next, the experience of apostle and
believer, which in the New Testament seized on the
Christ of the flesh, whom they had once known as
the finest and greatest of prophets, and which
identified Him with the ever-present Holy Spirit
in a realism more poignant than the tragedy of
life. They found in Christ not their consummation but their redemption, not their symbol but
their Saviour, not their ideal but their Redeemer,
not their guide but their life, not their comfort but
their justification. They were not His brothers
but His property. They found in Christ, not the
reflection upon the sky of their inward best, but
the invasion by God of their hopeless worst.

They found not cheer so much as mercy, not encouragement but forgiveness, not improvement and refinement but regeneration. They never think of finding themselves in Him but of finding God, never of finding self-realisation but always of finding divine revelation, not even of finding God so much as being found by Him. Christ did not in His person prolong their spiritual humanity into the heavenliest places, but He had to enter their souls and give them a quite new and revolutionised life. He had to create them anew by the gift of the Holy Ghost. An idea does not set up or restore life communion with God in the lost. He had to transcend in them all the historic influences that had made them, yea, even His own, felt merely as historic, and to become the Lord the Spirit, who acted on them, indeed, through history and its experience, but also in that very action, worked on them direct from God in a mediated immediacy. When they were bound into a community it was not that a church-spirit might assist them, but because the Holy Spirit had quite renewed them. Impressions from Christ were replaced by possession by Christ. And to live in Christ meant much more than living in his atmosphere as we might live in Tennyson's or Wesley's; it meant that He became their life and replaced their own.

It is this element, this new creative element, of personal redemption and regeneration that is the missing thing in the mystic-liberal type of religion which I began by describing. It has not as much power to convert and to create new life as some of the impossible orthodoxies. This is a lack that may be little felt by its subjects (though it is freely admitted by many of its impartial friends). The type may suffice for the quiet and normal experiences of an ordered, intelligent, and cultured life, whose interests are comparatively small and kindly, its sympathies more or less domestic or local, and its passions well in hand. Only when it faces the world problem in its passion, majesty, depth, and horror does it become so inadequate, like a maid in a mob, a yacht in a war, or a gull in a gale. And while it would be felt almost an abuse of terms to describe it as dangerous, yet dangerous it is, in the sense in which amiable people are dangerous in control of a stern situation and ' good fellows are bad officers.' *Summi adversarii nostri sunt suaves theologi.* There is a sense in which even fine spirituality and moral earnestness are dangerous to the Gospel ; and certainly there have been true mystics and strong prophets who have renounced and assailed it. These half truths and genial virtues can be dangerous to the Gospel (which means to Christ)

when they announce themselves as the whole ;
when they declare in words, or prove within the
limits of an individual life of inherited goodness, that they are independent of the Gospel, or
even hampered by it ; and when they lead people
winningly to think of the Gospel as but one of
many influences which produce the same excellent
and standard effect. The case of George Eliot the
positivist with her more than admiration for the
Imitation of Christ, or the case of Martineau with
his devotion to many like Richard Baxter, shows
that altruism of a Christian temper, or piety of
a Christian shade, may suffice for the personal
uses of many who are really upborne upon the
tradition of a society and a church resting on
far more positive and abysmal foundations. But
the mystic-liberal type does not suffice for a view,
far less for a treatment, of a world so tragic,
sinful, guilty, and desperate as history shows man's
moral case to be. And especially does this
discipleship-religion, this bloodless purity, this
piety so kindly pious, and this faith so gently
faithful, disqualify for any construction of this
raging world which does justice to holiness and
guilt, to the Cross and all its great train of effect,
thought, and experience in the conscience resist-
ing unto blood and saved as by fire. If there be
no sense or faith of a decisive and new creative

invasion of our personal life by God in Christ, but only a response by us to our affinity in Him ; if there be no experience of a judging and saving revelation in Christ but rather of a spiritual evolution ; then we are without a key to God's tragic and solemn relation to a world whose sin, perhaps, we are too pure to feel, whose misery we are too comfortable, and whose horrible guilt we are too placid to taste. If we have no real and critical revelation of God to our soul and conscience, then we have no ground in experience for recognising His great and crucial moral revelation in nature and history. The supernatural and the superhistoric on a world scale do not come home to us without the key of a crucial salvation from death to life, a real regeneration, and a new creation in the Holy Spirit. Such at least is the case with the Church as a whole. One does not of course expect the great dogmatic content of the Church to be reproduced in the experience of every member of it. That is a fertile source of forced piety and hectic faith. But, however it may be with individual cases, a church whose corporate and classic experience does not know the new creation in the Spirit, and a real conversion from the evolutionary progress even of a religion, can be no real witness of the supernatural in nature or the superhistoric in time. It is therefore a church incapable of serving Christ's purpose of a gospel for the world, or of promoting His kingdom, however it may revere His memory, own His greatness, or even adorn His teaching.

Therefore, I repeat, the test to which Congregationalism is being exposed does not concern its power to show a fine spirituality, or a keen philanthropy, or a zeal for social reform. But it is the question whether it is a capable trustee for God and man of anything so searching, critical, and revolutionary, so creative, universal, and eternal as the Gospel committed to the Church in the New Testament is. It is whether we can remain a Church of the Spirit that wields the Word for the world, or are doomed to subside into a large and promiscuous society of beneficent but insular spirituality—which spirituality in the next cycle ebbs to religious good form, while its beneficence sinks to genial good-will, and the cross becomes a Christmas tree.

LECTURE X

I HAVE been speaking of the religious, theological, and ecclesiastical features of Independency; but something remains to be said about the continuity of that public action which we have also seen to be such a distinctive note of its history. I have hinted that perhaps its lack of organisation handicaps it in dealing with social problems; while its tradition suggests rather political interests, and social questions chiefly as these increasingly become political. It becomes more and more difficult to say what the precise form of the Church's contribution to social questions should be. Its gospel certainly has social consequences, and a social ethic. It is the Church's business to teach accordingly. But how far is it its business to force any social programme for legislative effect? How far should it pass beyond loving sympathy, moral demands, and slow education in such things? How far can it lay down planks in a social platform? How far should it bring direct pressure to bear on legislation? Does or can the Church as such

254

know enough to urge a minimum wage by bounty-
fed industry ?   Social problems are now mostly
economic.   They are very complex, and call for
special knowledge and experience.   They are being
taken up more and more by Christian men, specially selected and organised for the purpose.   They
belong to a whole class of questions which once
were controlled by the Church but now more
properly pass to the State, or to society combined
for the purpose in voluntary action.   Is it asked
that in a great economic question, like the current
strikes, where two huge interests pull apart and go
to war, the Church shall place itself on one side of
the tug against the other ?   Would that not be
like giving one of them the benefit of a black
military ?   Certainly there is a kind of economic
issue where the Church has a right to intervene
with a strong and urgent opinion.   The working
classes, we are told, are interested at present in
little but wages—not in politics—in a larger share
of what they go to make.   Who can wonder ?   But
the wage question is twofold.   It may concern a
living wage to all, even the least skilled, the demand
that a man should enjoy the fruit of his labour to
an extent that enables him to live under cheerful
family conditions without hardship, poverty, and
strain.   Or, when that minimum has been reached,
it may concern a share, which is just on other

grounds, of the profit which skilled labour enables capital to make. In the latter case the Church has little call to interfere. It is a matter of the market, and of collective bargaining which need not be less friendly than other business. But in the former case the Church has both a right and a duty to speak. In the interest of the moral personality it must urge that the practical people shall so re-arrange things that profitable industry shall not rest on a foundation which in some ways is worse than slavery—worse because the slaves were well fed as pieces of property, and tended as machines. But I do not know any church, certainly any free church, that does not hold that doctrine, and does not express it by its representative men and assemblies as soon as the facts become certain and clear. But the Church is asked to cast itself collectively into a fray, and take a side when the crisis has become acute. Well, even that is not more than might properly be expected if the oppressed side was helpless, and had no more effective champion or weapon. But the power and right of labour to combine under moral conditions provides it with a weapon more effectual than a charitable championship from without. It can develop from its own interior men who are better able to manage its case for reform than the ministers at least can do

who specially represent the Church and its regeneration. And the entry of the Church on
the actual arena has often been met with contempt or ridicule more or less polite from one side
or the other. On the other hand, the more the
Church refuses to go down into the party clash,
so much the more explicit she should be in her
moral guidance to those who do. And so much
the more should she rouse the conscience of those
who, having done well out of the existing order
of things, are much too content with it, and
ignobly hostile to its change.

The public question of the hour is the question of
poverty. It is a question which it will take the
combined resources of all sections of society to
solve. And it is a question in which the Church
has a hereditary right. The Church spread faster,
though not deeper, at the very first by its willing
ministration to poverty with such wisdom as the
age allowed. Its unparaded ministries to the poor
have run alongside its more ostentatious energies
all the way like a mountain stream by a bustling
road. The monasteries sheltered beneficence as
well as pomp and idleness, and they came to their
power and pomp by it. When the modern economic age began, capitalism was taken charge of by
the Calvinism in which Independency grew ; and

R

it became the great means by which opportunity
was found for the worker and help for the poor.
It has made the conditions in which labour is
rising to power, and maintaining its own cause, as
capital did against *its* feudal foes. True, the richest
grow very rich and the poorest very poor, though
the workers in the mass are better off than ever;
yet the standard of living has recently been rising
faster than their means, and, quite recently, prices
rising on a fixed wage. And, besides the standard
of comfort, there has been rising the standard of
justice and of the labourer's right to a larger share
in the fruit of his toil. The extremes are acute,
and it is the present business of society to adjust
that tension, and of the Church to press the adjustment as a duty. And the Church as a whole
(I am not speaking of individuals or groups) does
not make a secret where its sympathies lie when the
facts are clear. But it would be a poor service to
poverty if the Church were to win a victory for it,
and make it a present of the victory, when it can
enable and encourage it to win it for itself.

One finds political speakers often calling on the
Church, as it values its life, to come to the social
rescue; but I do not recall one who gives it an
informed programme, or who sees that the real
unity of the Church for social or any reform
cannot rest upon its combination against abuses

or wrongs. Though of course more in the Church
should be active, as more of the working classes
should be living up to the labour ideal. Many
seem to think that if the Church is not on the
ground for social reform it has no reason to exist
at all. To all such it should plainly be said that,
while the Church must do much for social reform,
that is not the chief end of the Church. Its work
for its chief end it must settle for itself. The out-
sider has no right to prescribe. A particular programme, presented for its acceptance at the peril
of unpopularity, may not be the line of action its
own judgment may prescribe; the adoption of it is
not necessarily the article of a standing or falling
church. The supernatural mission of the Church
is always prime. If the representative of the
Church cannot speak for the working class as
their own experts and orators can do, neither
can these speak and judge for the Church, especially from outside of it and its first charge in
its Gospel. The Church can only speak to any
purpose when it is regarded by either side as a
real adviser and not as a useful asset. And on
the whole that is not how any church is regarded
when war is declared.

But the service of the Church to the social
problem is much deeper, and more vital; it is

less obvious, less direct than the order for the
day, and therefore less welcome. It must provide
a satisfaction for the supreme and aching need of
society in all ranks, for the moral need everywhere,
the need of a habitual authority, final at once for
the individual and for society, which it is man's
glory to own and his prosperity to serve. The lack
of this is dissolving society. The age of the conflict
for liberty is practically drawing to a close. Liberty
has in the main been secured. Its cause at least is
safe. The problem is not to win it, but, having got
it, to use it. What are we to do with it ? How
is it to be kept from disintegrating society, how
made the large atmosphere of its consolidation and
progress ? Capital and Labour are equally free to
combine, so far as public liberty is concerned. It
is an immense power, charged with as much possibility for destruction as for construction. Have we
imagination enough to forecast the consequences of
impatient action on a large scale, or docility enough
to listen to those who do ? Is the power held with
any due sense of its responsibility ? What is to
furnish a conscience for it ? What or whom is it
chiefly to serve ? To what solemn authority does
it go which can guide a power so great and terrible ?
For the press this means nothing. But in action and
in belief the supreme need of the hour is an authority, a living conscience universal, nay eternal, a real

King of Humanity, with a first claim to be wor-
shipped and obeyed, and not simply to be utilised in
the junctures of life, whose holy will and loving purpose every human ideal must serve and glorify. Our
supreme need is a holy and actual God, of the most
intimate and eternal relevancy to Humanity, with
power to love to the uttermost, but also to secure
to the end His purpose of love, to secure it step
by step in history, to raise the weak, war down the
proud, judge to the last farthing, save to the last
soul, and reign and rule for ever and ever. A God
we need, Whose whole reason for existence is not
simply to serve, indulge, and aggrandise Humanity
till it behave like a spoilt child, but Who exists
to make His free service, honour, and worship
man's chief end, his first care, and his final crown.
That is the supreme need of the hour—to provide
and secure in practical effect amid human affairs
that Lord as not only our Saviour but also our
daily Master and Majesty. And that is the need
the Church alone meets. To bring and establish
in men's hearts and business such a God is the
Church's commission from Himself, and the last
and greatest service it can render to mankind.
The Church alone has a Gospel of which it can say
that if every man received it and obeyed it social
questions would solve themselves. If that Gospel is
rejected then of course the Church must be scorned.

And what has it else at last ?   Humanity can look after its own progress, but it cannot provide its own God nor save its own soul.   And when the last pinch comes it is by God we live and progress, and by such a God, and not by bread alone.   The first society the Gospel has to consider is the Church it created, in which all society is to be blessed.

Let me return to this by a large curve, but all in the context of the chief interest of these pages.

It is said with truth that Independency has thrown entirely away the Calvinism in which it arose.   Last century it passed, through an eclectic kind of Arminianism, to a religion of Fatherhood in which Christ holds a vital place, though one variously construed as more or less close.   But there would be an almost unanimous repudiation of Puritan Calvinism ; and the works of its divines are as unsaleable as a diamond-field at the North Pole, or a gold mine under the Atlantic.   It is not perhaps quite clear to most what it is that is rejected.   For some Calvinism means no more than it does to the *littérateur*—it is a portmanteau word for all in Christianity that makes a demand for positive belief, or is outside the interests of current sentiment.   But most people, if pressed, would probably say that the intolerable thing in Calvinism was the doctrine of predestination.

Even there there is often some lack of lucidity.
The objector does not object to believe that God
has chosen *him* to eternal life and goodness, or
that his moral hope is in the individualised love
of God. *Aimer c'est choisir*, always. And if he
observes what is going on abroad he may see that
some of the most pronounced liberals are returning
to a fresh interest in the doctrine, as one that cannot
be entirely got rid of in any reasoned view of God's
relation to man—even if you regard nothing more
than the inequalities of society. But what would
probably be most unfamiliar to him is this, that the
essence of Calvinism is not the doctrine of predestination but the doctrine of God—which is
indeed the essence and characteristic of every
religion, and of every great version of it. (The
triune God, for instance, is what makes Christianity
Christian.) Predestination was in this respect a
means rather than an end. It was the only means
that Calvin, or Augustine either, saw for giving
effect to the supreme end, which is the absolute
freedom and majesty of God in the course of
history. Let what may become of man's freedom,
they said, nothing must impair the absolute freedom
of God's grace. *Our* first concern to-day is really
a secondary one—how man can be free with such
a sovereign God ; but Calvin's was the primary
concern—how God can be free with such men.

Calvinism did so much for man's freedom because
it would first have God's at any price to man, and
would secure the glory of God even if most men
were a shame. To provide for this supreme
interest Calvin, like so many of the world's first
minds, saw no other means than a certain doctrine
of predestination. But the immortal service of
Calvin to faith has not been his means, but the
persistent supremacy of his end. It is the reduction of man to serve the freedom and worship the
glory of a holy, loving, and absolute God.

And to this must we not return ? From this have
we not strayed towards chaos ? We Independents
in particular, who can never resume our great
founder's form of predestination—can we not, should
we not, recover his idea of God as absolute Lord ?
With our extreme sensibility to the movements of
each age, have we not become the victims of the
humanism, the subjectivism, the atomism, of the last
several generations ? Is that not the secret of our
waning hold upon humanity ? Human nature in the
end yields more in the long run to those who command it than to those who indulge it, to a prophet
of God with his word ' Repent ' than to a tribune
of man with his word ' Expand.' Have we not
joined those who regard God as man's first asset
rather than man as God's first subject and servant ?
Have we not taught men to think of Him as their

lover and benefactor forgetting their King, as the
fount of an infinite pity rather than the Father of an
infinite holy majesty ? Does that not mean that
we have had more to say about God being wholly
at man's service than about man being absolutely
at God's ? Is that not the reason why we find it so
difficult to get service for God ? Is it not because
we are always accustoming man to think first of
himself, with God to wait on him and his ideals ?

Must the Church not return, with or without us, to
Calvin's idea of God, which indeed is the idea of the
Bible and of Revelation ? Did Christ not save man
by first glorifying God ? Is a new Calvinism not
part of the true Catholicity ? Must we not do, if not
less to win the democracy for the Church, more to
glorify the God who saves it ? In the failure of
our effort to win the democracy must not all the
churches go back to a more close and prime concern for the God who alone can win it, and for the
revelation that alone can save it—back to at least
as much concern for God's truth as for human
welfare, which can only stand on that truth, and
prosper as we magnify it ? Does not the threatening
and anarchic state of society—when we are unsure
whether the great providential calamity which is to
bring us to our senses will be war with a foreign power
or a civil war more bitter and no less deadly than the
stricken field—does not the state of society indicate

that the gospels of the last century have failed—
orthodox or heterodox—and that the hour needs
another, if it be not yet too late ? Is it not the hour
when we should have, not indeed less to say about
a ministering God, but more about a ruling God,
not less about a healing God, but more about an
authoritative God, not less about a Gospel that
blesses, but more about a Gospel that commands,
judges, humbles, and awes ? If we did preach in
word and deed a God like that, should we not be
more true to ourselves and our source, to our genius
and our genesis, than if we pursued the empty
phantom of an absolute liberty without an absolute
Lord, and a free Spirit without a final Word ?

The Christianity of a great mass of cultivated
Christian people might perhaps be described as
Christian Personalism, the culture of personality
by means of Christianity, and the culture of the
kind of Christianity that best lends itself to that
purpose. It is a conspicuous feature of that lay
religion which deserves so much more study from
those who aim at understanding the Christian
public than it receives. One excellent quality this
ethical type of religion has. It is in protest against
the external culture, the mere civilisation, which has
taken such violent possession of the age—the passion
merely to master and enjoy the world, with all the

facilities thereto that applied science or social opportunity lends. Something is still to be said, it is felt, for applied religion. Culture by all means, but not the culture of science nor of art, but moral culture ; and moral culture with all the aids lent it by religion, and notably by the most ethical of all religions, by Christianity. Material culture must be corrected, enlarged, and saved by moral culture of an idealist kind. Many of the most influential writers, philosophers, and theologians of the day are of this stamp. They turn from naturalism, and the grosser realism, and the elaborate machinery for comfort and enjoyment. The only real thing for them is personality, the only real religion the cult of personality. Christianity is the religion of ethical culture. They psychologise on the subject, they spiritualise. They are not Monistic. They have a firm yet large grasp of the personality of God ; and they cling to it as the chief guarantee of man's personality and its culture. Their object of life is the creation and development of personality, under such an influence as religion in chief. Their goal is the perfecting of that moral organism ; and that perfection is an instinct which it shares with every other living thing. Everything in life (including often God Himself) is held to be there for this service. It is all material for this high—shall we call it ?—egocentricity.

The highest types of this tendency come very near us, and seem to many to be quite within the kingdom of Heaven. They recognise, as some one points out, two supreme obstacles to this personal perfection on which all life should be set—the laming power of sin in the will, and the dooming power of guilt in the conscience. This bondage, this guilt must be destroyed. The conscience must be forgiven, the will must be renewed. The personality is choked and hampered at every turn till this is done.

What is the real ruling interest in this high and attractive scheme ? What most fills the mind of those who cherish it ? Is it God or man ? Is it the holiness of God and its due, or the moral career of man and its due ? Is it God's sanctity or man's moral dignity ? Does man supremely serve the right and majesty of God, or does God serve the absorbing moral ideality of man ?

They turn to Christ. Indeed they seldom turn away from Him. He comes to fill their ideal world. Here is the supreme case of the moral personality perfectly realised and overcoming the world. Could we but be perfect as He is perfect. Here is the mighty man of soul, the grand symbol of spiritual manhood, the apotheosis of all the faith which crowns character, and which we but feebly win. But Christ is for them the divine subject of faith not its object, the great exponent of

our faith not its recipient. He is the chief hero, or
the symbol, of human kindness, ethical sanctity, and
ideal religion. In Him we do not meet God, but
only the greatest of all who have met God. He represents not God manifest in the flesh so much as
God appreciated in the Spirit. Beyond that Soul's
attitude to God faith cannot go. But as to God's
attitude to the soul, even Christ is not absolutely final
—since in Him we have man's supreme grasp of
God rather than God's supreme grasp of man. God,
revelation, is still in the rear ; what is to the fore
is man, faith, sanctification, self-realisation. God
reveals Himself for man's moral aid and perfecting,
for character not for the kingdom, for such a creation as Christ was, not for anything which God
owes primarily to His own holy and awful name. Redemption is all, atonement is nothing. Thus Jesus,
as the perfection of faith, even comes between
them and a ruling God. God is apt to be regarded
as but the divine means for that ideal human end.
Religion takes the place of God in the subtlest way,
and we are tempted with the most angelic light.
" We have a theology, brilliant as never before
in all that concerns insight into the humane and
genial aspect of religion, and rich in its power to
divine the divine in the many creeds of earth ; but
one that is really an anthropology rather than a
theology, being more engrossed with the divine side

of man than immersed in the deep things of God."
Just as the worldling loses God in His gifts so this
view of things loses God in His graces, in His fruit
in man. We are skilful in the philology of the book
of History, but we are to seek in its exegesis, and
nowhere in its theology. God is apt to be sunk in
history, and in the triumphs and spiritualities of the
soul, just as, for many on a lower stage, He is lost
in nature. Not that His power is not felt in nature,
any more than His effect is unfelt in the classic
creeds of the prophetic souls. But practically these
religions are in front and He is behind. They engross
us as He does not. He has the courtesy rank, they
have the real. Just as in our provincial towns
there are philosophical societies in which never a.
word of philosophy is heard, the rudimentary terms
of it are not understood, and all has dropped to
physical science of a more or less amateur kind;
so we have works, journals, and chairs in theology
which are absorbed, and often successfully and even
brilliantly absorbed, in history, but strangely shy
and unfamiliar in the region of such theology as
unravels God's revelation of His ultimate nature,
purpose, and thought. They cultivate or even
parade a dogmatic indifference, a theological
agnosticism. We are not irreligious, but we are
not Christian. The whole type of our religion is
anthropocentric instead of theocentric; it is more

concerned with the growing personality of man
than with the holy personality of God. Therefore
God's love itself becomes a powerless thing, moving
eloquence more than action, touching us when it
should humble us, and wooing where it should
make us wince. And the person of Christ becomes
then but ill understood. For it has been well said
that God's love becomes for us a reality only in the
Godhead of Jesus Christ, which, the lay Christian
is apt to think and ready to say, is not a thing he
can or need understand. Whereas it is the one thing
he must understand, and it must be made capable
of being understood by him, if a Christian he is to
remain, or his children. I will not say it is meaningless in such a case to speak of God's love, but it
lacks the chief thing which needed to be secured,
and which Christ came to establish about that love
—its reality, its certainty, its holiness, its majesty,
and its secure triumph in the race. Such partial
triumph as it has is only in souls, or a group of
souls. It is not asserted over the whole of creation,
the whole of nature. God subdues the soul, but
He does not command the world. Like the reflex
action of prayer, it is a victory subjective to faith,
it is faith's reaction on the soul ; it is not objective,
not mastering, for creation and all the powers
therein that war upon the soul. It is tempted to
dismiss Christ's miracles on nature by comparison

with His personal effect on souls. But without the miracles and resurrection of Christ the theodicy is incomplete—certainly the eschatology is. The groaning of creation is not stilled. It was not the whole of Christ's work to create a kingdom of souls whose moral elevation should transcend all the ills that flesh is heir to, and lose in elation the sense of them. The miracles that controlled Nature have a larger revelation than that—imposing as that is. They are harbingers of the restoration of all things, and preludes of the time when all things are palpably to work together for those that are called in God's purpose of love. The human fruition of God's love is not all. There is, besides, its almighty power on creation, which groans and travails with the holy consummation. There is God's purpose with the creation as a whole—which is there to glorify God and justify Him for ever. That is man's chief end—to enjoy Him, indeed ; but in the concent of a creation uttering His self-justification after all for having made it. The supreme object of life is neither to perfect the soul nor to enjoy God, but so to finish the work given us to do as to justify and glorify Him for ever. And our quest must be by what life or death we should glorify God.

There is a widespread sense, even among those who all their life have magnified the love of God,

and have done so at the expense, often, of everything else divine, that there is something wrong
in the message. Or less wrong, perhaps, than inadequate and short. It does not reach. It is
ineffectual. It lacks something. It is short of the
fulness, the urgency, the compulsion, the incision of
the Gospel. It lacks practical effect on character,
even when character is the standard. A gospel
of nothing but love does not produce character.
Is it not just because something so subjective as
character is the standard, because we have our eye
on our moral selves and our needs more than on the
holy God and His dues, because of something that
is not given us even in the character of Christ,
something not revealed except in the cross of Christ ?
It is felt that there is in the conception of God's
love, and especially in the more modern gospels of
it, something one-sided, something over-obvious
and therefore weak. God's love is too much a
matter of course, too facile in Him, to arrest people.
It does not make them wonder and fear. It is
just paternity transfigured, maternity taken up to
heaven. There is a soft and cheap strain in it
which unfits it for the moral task of seizing and
rearing personality in a mighty history like man's.
An element has gone out of it whose absence makes
half the Bible meaningless—the element of holiness,
majesty, and judgment. Love is thus preached as

a means instead of an end, as a moral means instead
of an absolute worship, as a means for personal
culture, self-realisation, and finishing the soul's
pyramid. It is love finely egoistic, but egoistic
still; and therefore, in so far, morally impotent,
and unequal to the final consummation of a race
of souls made for God's purpose before their own
perfection. The matter of guilt is not dealt with.
It is put aside. We are invited to forget it, and
not brood too much on it; to forget it in a hopeful
courage within ourselves, and in the culture of love
from soul to soul; for which good cheer we have
Christ as sufficient ground. But is the love of God
revealed to us in the New Testament chiefly as the
great means for our personal culture or cheer, moral
and spiritual? Are we not here for that God
more even than that God for us? Can we wonder
that religion becomes trivial when the matter of
revelation is so belittled, and God is made to serve
thus? Can we wonder that it loses solemn fear
and deep humility, and the note of obedience?
It loses the effect of God's self-surrender in Christ
because it loses the sense of the greatness He
surrendered. Christ has not the dynamic of the
triune God. Guilt comes to be felt as a disorder
in us instead of a wound to the holy majesty of
God. And the cross of Christ is treated as the great
means of our peace, or of harmonising our life by

the spirit of sacrifice ; whereas, because God is God upon all the floods, it is the judgment which re-establishes His holy righteousness on the riot of our sin by an act as awful, real, and historic as the sin itself.

Many fine, ideal, and earnest spirits take God's love much too lightly ; and we feel a certain shock of contrast between their own earnestness and the comparative levity of the message they bring. There is a conjunction of the serious personalism I spoke of and a certain—well perhaps levity is a term too heavy—a poverty, and futility. It leaves many a Christian with what might be called but a young and mettled faith, given to military methods and metaphors, an unbroken, untamed, unsearched faith, a forthright, cheery, self-certain and self-respecting faith, which savours more of old Stoicism or a young colony than of the broken, shamed, and contrite spirit which finds itself not in personal development or culture but only in an absolute salvation. As if Christ came but to promote moral excellence, service, and happiness, and the offence and tragedy of the Cross had now ceased.

The cult of culture has invaded Christianity too far when it reduces the cross of the Eternal Son of God to no more than a means of spiritual discipline and the production of character. Personalism of that kind is certainly a part of our sanctification.

But it was not solely, not directly, for such ethical sanctification that Christ lived and died. Our sanctification itself grows from our redemption. It is the evolution of our justification. And we must orient our experience anew, from the centre provided in the Cross as the self-justification of God, and the atonement He made to His own Holy Name at the moral heart of all being. A living relation to Christ's Person there must be ; but also it must be, or tend to be, a deeper relation still to His Cross as the core, crisis, and achievement of His person. Otherwise there is danger of Christianity, in some of its most worthy and attractive forms, becoming a religion of moral culture and spiritual æsthetic. Christianity is not cultured spirituality, but a new creation. Discipleship is well, but it was not discipleship that conquered the world for Christ, it was apostleship. It was not a disciple church but an apostolic, a church not of Christian learners but of Christian confessors. Since the decisive things of the Cross, the Tomb, and Pentecost, the Christian is much more than a disciple of Christ—he is a member of Christ ; he is a confessor and a regenerate. Discipleship is no match for the degeneration and egotism which are in the world by lust. We are not now Christ's disciples merely but His purchased property ; and Christianity before it is a discipline is a salvation. It is not the religion of spiritual personality, but of moral redemption by atoning forgiveness and sanctification by the Holy Ghost. Christ is more than Master or Brother; He is made to us justification, and sanctification, and redemption. And above all He is our Lord God with something more than a *value* for us—with an eternal and costly *right* whose value we but poorly prove.

One thing let me make clear, to avert a despotic idea of God's Lordship. It is not the Lordship of a mere imperative, even of the moral imperative idealised, but of a triumphant teleology, the vast Amen. The great moral motive after all is less a command than an ideal, and it is most of all a practical consummation. An ideal kindles us more mightily and effectively than a decree; and an ideal which is a purpose, and not a purpose only but a universal purpose already achieved and victorious, does so most of all. Such is the moral majesty of God—God not as the Eternal Imperative of the conscience but as its Everlasting Redeemer. His absolute royalty is founded in His absolute and finished salvation of the whole world. And the centre of majesty has passed, since Calvin, from the decrees of God to His Act, to the foregone establishment in Christ's Cross of a moral Kingdom without end, which is the key and goal of history.

LECTURE XI

THE NEW CALVINISM—II

THERE is a practical illustration of the way in which a humanitarian or anthropocentric conception of God defeats its own end, and threatens practical atheism. I refer to the attitude of the working classes to the churches.

The reference is to the working class because it is the class which at the moment is fighting for its footing in the economic conflict. But had the same conception of God been the prevalent one when the middle class was engaged in the like battle, what I say would have applied equally to it. It is, however, a peculiarity of the present situation that the rise of the democracy coincides with the modern anthropocentric idea of God as tributary to man ; whereas the upper and middle classes secured their position under a different conception—one which regarded man as there for obedience to God rather than God for the service of man. The rise of the middle class, especially, took place under the influence of Calvinism, in which there is no question as to the theocentric place of man rather than the anthropocentric place of God. God is certainly there for man, but only with the purpose of putting man there for God. The present struggle of the democracy is the first great class struggle that has taken place under the humanitarian idea of God.

What then is the action of the idea upon the working classes to whom it comes ? What they are told is that the chief value of God to man is as a helper ; and if He is offered as a saviour it means mostly a saviour either from the consequences of sin, or from the poor, or even wretched, conditions under which they live, and especially from poverty. And of course that is so. Christ's God is such a God. But is He that first and last ? Was that Christ's *raison d'etre* here ? Is that all He is ? Is He there to make the most of man at any price ? An overfond mother may sacrifice everything to make prosperity and position for her son, only to be heart-broken when she finds she bores him, when he refuses to see her because he is too busy, or has a party of his great friends, or when he finally disowns her because he needs her no more. Is that the fond nature and fatal outcome of God's Father-hood ? Does it only give, foster, and fortify ? Of course when I draw it out so, and so illustrate it, those who offer such a God repudiate the idea. But that is simply because they pursue it no farther than its sentimental aspect, or its benevolent utility. They are sometimes without moral insight or imagination. But the practical effect of such a God is, in the long run, no other than my parable indicates. The race becomes pauperised, exacting, and intractable. This must always be the practical effect of a God who is God to us only because of His value, and not because of His right, only because He helps us and not because He rules us, only because He asks sympathy and not obedience. The Church is suffering much because it has preached a salvation from sin's consequences instead of from sin, from what a man suffers than from what he is and does. Is it not another phase of the same fallacy when we offer a God whose chief use to man is to supply him with a living rather than a loyalty, and abolish poverty regardless of guilt ?

Mr. Bernard Shaw, for instance, has this passage (preface to *Major Barbara*) :—

' The crying need of the nation is not for better morals, cheaper bread, temperance, liberty, culture, redemption of fallen sisters and erring brothers, nor the grace, love, and fellowship of the Trinity ; but simply for enough money. And the evil to be attacked is not sin, suffering, greed, priestcraft, kingcraft, demagogy, monopoly, ignorance, drink, war, pestilence, nor any other of the scapegoats which reformers sacrifice, but simply poverty.'

Of course what Mr. Shaw means behind all this is that the social question is now for the time an

economic question. We all know that ; but we are
not all literary, and we distrust literary effect and
the narrow unreality it is prone to ; and many of us
know the last Reality well ; and we are familiar with
huge sections of society which are to Mr. Shaw a
closed book ; and we have access to human hearts
which shut to the coming of his cynic wit and
wilful paradox acting with a slash

' Wie ein Knabe
Der Disteln köpft ' ;

and we know better than to gird either at the
kindest philanthropy or the most solemn religion
—without which the poverty of the country would
have had the heads off the class Mr. Shaw belongs
to long ago.   We know that the economic question
is not the only social question, nor indeed the chief,
if we go farther back in moral realism than Mr.
Shaw's divining power can carry him.   Nor is
the social question the only one—unless where it
is said that the only personal relations in existence
are those between man and man, and we have none
with a living God of an everlasting and exigent
righteousness.

The passage is quite characteristic of Mr. Shaw's
hard and monocular vision as a pedant of actuality ;
and it places him in the same mental category as
the orthodoxists who preach no more than a salvation from hell.   They have both the same order of
moral mind, only in the one case it takes a theo-

logical in the other a social form. Both live in a
moral world without atmosphere, and see things
without sky or perspective (which is another way
of saying that neither has the historic or evolutionary sense of society). Both are prophets of views
without vision, and judgment without insight.
Both represent a loveless prophetism—a prophetism
with the bottom knocked out. Which of us does
not feel how much truth is in Mr. Shaw's thought
—and how false it is, how false in the matter of
moral realism ; how skilful he is with his finger on
a spot, and how utterly unable he is to envisage
a moral universe ; how he can diagnose a disease
in a mechanical way without any power to understand the constitution of the patient ; and how
deft and cocksure he is with his surgery as the
last word in the case. It is no wonder, however,
that Mr. Shaw, with his literary skill and grotesque
wit, has much vogue with the Socialism that feels
things to be wrong without heart enough to feel
how wrong, without heart, in the Bible use of the
word, with a heart for man's suffering from man
but none for God's. There are crowds and crowds
of even Christian people who are sympathetic for
every human ache (who are even tempted by the
passion of their sympathy to challenge the patient
sympathy of God), who have a heart for every
plea of man, but they are entirely heartless for

the affliction of the God of a prodigal race with the iniquity of it all laid upon His holy Soul.

If the working class could understand Mr. Shaw they too would mostly find such a passage as I quoted a great relief in the way of expressing their feelings. And they would have much to say for themselves. They are not properly paid compared with other classes. Comfort and happiness are ill apportioned in life. And unrest and renovation must go on, till the remediable part of such a state of things is put right in a spirit of anxious equity. But is that the worst that ails the world ? When comfort is equalised is the world right with the last moral reality ? When society hums with culture, and teems with civilisation, and the great human machine is working at full pressure, and with the joy of its harmonious powers—then shall the end be ? When God, or the belief in a God, has done all that such a power, or such an idea, can do to develop man's resource and satisfaction, may He, may it, be pensioned ? Is a living relation of absolute obedience to a living God whose right it is to reign for ever and ever—is that irrelevant to the final purpose and the glorious destiny of Humanity ? Yet if God is only the supreme and solemn utility why should he continue to be regarded with more than passing gratitude at best when the end has been reached ? If He is there chiefly to help to realise human ideals, and is valuable chiefly to that end, where is His value, His place, when the end is reached ? When man is his own king and providence shall the kingship of God be kept but in a museum ?

The practical result of the humanitarian idea, of God of which I spoke appears expressly in the attitude and address of many of the working class to the churches. 'Have you a God who commands you to put your resources wholly at the service of the humanitarian ideas for which we stand ? If not, we have no use for you ; nor for any God who does not. You and your God are of use to the world only as they promote our ideals. For we are the vanguard of Humanity, nay, the tribunal ; and we represent to-day the chief and only cause of a humane God. The world, history, is resolved into one great battle. This battle is the divine Armageddon. This is the Lord's real controversy. We stand on one side, our opponents on the other. And we stand for the Lord's side. God's supreme interest in the world or the soul is that the victory should be ours. If you do not join us you are a false church with a false God. You are on the world's side and not on God's, not on Christ's.'

I confess I am not surprised when I hear the Trades Unionists, and especially the Socialists, talk like that. It is just what a man like Mr. Keir Hardie might be expected to say, what he ought to say, what the humanitarian anthropocentric God of the churches of last century compels him to say. There is no doubt in my mind that the best social interests of Humanity at the moment do lie along the line which gives the working people what they have not yet—their due share in the products of their labour and the blessings of society. And if the supreme function of a God is to advance Humanity, to develop and adjust its social resources, and to beam upon the prospect of some closing cycle rich in public good and personal culture ; if the supreme function of a God is to be such a helper, such a benefactor, such a saviour, such a promoter of humane ideals in every direction—if that is what a God is there for, then such language to the Church from the working class is entirely in place. The working class is turning upon the Church with fair effect the idea of God the pulpit has been promoting—the kind Father. The Church of such a God, if it be the supreme organ of God's purpose on earth, should place itself and all its resources on the democratic side, and enter the arena of the class war in force. He is not then the Lord and Judge of Labour exactly as He is of Capital.

The attitude of the working classes to the Church

is just what was bound to result from the God of a
mere social service, the God offered especially by
the churches nearest these classes for the last half
century at least; and happily offered, if it were
not made all.

But the God of the Church's revelation is not an
anthropocentric God.   Heaven is not Humanity
glorified, even by a God.   The public is not the
tribunal of the Church.   The revelation in Christ
entrusted to the Church reveals God for whom
man exists, rather than man for whom God
exists.   What God does for man is to replace
him in absolute obedience to God—the obedience
of entire trust and communing love.   The redemption is a redemption from all the cultures,
comforts, and happinesses, into the worship and
service of the Holy One who here and now
inhabits Eternity.   The Church is there not in
the first place for the service of man, but for his
service, witness, and worship of the God in Whose
holy love alone man comes to himself and achieves
his destiny.   All the development of Humanity,
all the adjustment of classes and of wealth, is
there for the final purpose of reconciling man's
soul to God; and the crown of human welfare is
that man should love and worship God for His
holy Self, and not as an asset of supreme value for
human weal.   Human weal is not assured till we

find it in forgetting about it by comparison with
our practical confession and communion of God's
holy love and glorious majesty and blessed kingdom. The Church is there to secure such a God
in man's heart and service, not to guarantee the
alliance of such a God with the human cause.

It has been a chivalrous feature in Independency
that it has always been to the front when it was
a case of rousing and helping a new movement of
the Spirit, or promoting a healthy reaction against
some idea which had done its work and outstayed
its use. The light-armed organisation of the
body, and its looseness to tradition, have made
such adaptation more easy; and its rapport with
the public gave it a quick sensibility for the new
movements while they were as yet in the air on
their wireless way. It has had a spiritual tele-
pathy, which yet had a very sound, positive
foundation, and a saving good sense in religious
things. It is a high virtue that, amid all its sympathy with the valuable novelties and liberties of
last century, as a body it should still be evangelical
both in creed and tone. It has shown a happy
insight and sound *flair* for the things that should be
shaken and the things that should remain. It has
been hospitable to the future, respectful to the past,
and faithful to the present. Its sympathies have

been true to both the old Gospel and the new
knowledge. It has not always seen their adjustment
(to-day that is often very hard to see) ; but it has
trusted One Who does see it and, what is more, Who
holds it, and, what is most, Who *is* the common
Peace. It is easy to harden up as champions to
the right hand or to the left ; it is not easy to
stand angelic with a foot on the land and one on
the sea, and having done all to stand. It had
been easy to stand where the eighteenth century
stood and not budge ; and it had been easy to
become fluid with the nineteenth and stand not
at all. But it has not been easy to stay rooted
like a great tree which yet is flexible to all winds,
and is more secure than a tower because it has
the power to yield. To the note of liberty which
filled last century Independency has responded
well. What is the new note, and how shall it
respond there ?

The new need created for the soul by its new
liberty is an authority. Liberty is most valuable
because it gives new value, new meaning and
opportunity to the true authority. The very
extravagances of liberty carry home to us new
resources in authority, a wider sense of its blessing, and a deeper note in its worship. They
enlarge to us the range of its noble rule. A century of the passion to be free only prepares for

another with the passion to serve, and the hunger
for a king. An age of pity is bound to rouse the
demand for an Almighty who is capable of *effective*
pity, and pity for a whole race. An age of reform
and redress is bound to set the soul upon asking
what provision there is to remedy the wrong that
runs through the heart of existence; and it stirs
the quest for a righteousness absolute and eternal,
in a word, holy. The more men learn to prize
love the more must they ask at last if man is
loved as men can love; and if he is loved with
a love so holy and mighty that it has the right
to command all, the grace to save all, and the
power to subdue all. The more we enlarge and
expand, so much the longer are the arms we
stretch to the throne, and the deeper is the prayer
we lift to its power. The more we may go where
we please the more we feel we need a guide, and
finally an obedience; being tired with an unchartered freedom and crushed with the load of
chance desires. If our late passion was liberty,
and our present is sympathy, our coming passion is
authority. But an authority which carries all blessing and freedom with it. It is an authority acting
in a sympathetic atmosphere of loyalty generated
in a social body of a Church. And it is an
authority of Gospel whose nature it is to create
freedom; for our freedom is one we do not win,

T

but it is given us by our absolute authority. OUR
GENIUS IS A FOUNDED FREEDOM.

This alters greatly the situation, and especially
for the Church. And it will give a great advantage
to such churches as are most freely sure of their
Gospel and their commission. Every church, in
so far as it is a true church, must welcome the
change which turns the question of the age from
a freedom to an authority that creates freedom.
For to every true church the note of authority
must be uppermost. To put liberty, which is a
secondary matter, before authority, which is a
primary and fontal even for liberty itself, is to
confess a sect and not a church.

Those who have had the patience to follow me
with any sympathy will not suggest that I think
for a moment of the authority of a church as
residing anywhere except in the message it has in
trust. It is not a case of prerogative or privilege—
in the common and sometimes unworthy sense of
such words. It is nothing of what Gladstone used
to call ' that base-born word prestige.' It is not
the prophet that commands but his Word, not the
priest but the sacrifice, not the Church but the
Cross, not the saint but the Saviour. The religion
of the eighteenth century was truly in dire need of
that note of sympathy and intimacy so freely

given it by the nineteenth. But no less does the nineteenth century need from the twentieth the restoration to Fatherhood of the idea of sovereignty, and to love its eternal holiness, whereby it not only suffers to save but suffers judgment and not grief alone. As I have said, pity and sympathy only become religious when they are joined to a righteousness which is almighty to save into its own holiness. Are the tears in things the tears over Jerusalem? Are they the tears of the Holy Love as Redeemer? Are they the sweat of the saving agony of Almighty God? We do not ask, is He willing to save, but, is He *able* to save, and to save to the uttermost? Has He more power to save than we have to feel? Has He more right to reign than we have to pray? Have we, perhaps, been inverting things? Has His love made Him more lovely to us than commanding? Does any one know what holiness is who is more sensible of the beauty of it than humbled with its majesty and abased with its judgment? Is it God's love when we are so affected by the kindness of it that we have lost power to feel its solemnity and cherish but a cheery faith? Is it the liberty in Christ when we feel more free than obedient, and more released than ruled? Yet to canonise liberty in place of sanctity is to come to that. It is a searching question for any church, ' Which

stirs your heart most—liberty or holiness ? ' And
a truthful answer might be crushing.

The word of the Church is not that of a merciful
God, but of a God who has power to make His
mercy conquer all for His holy glory in our joy.
It is a word of human freedom only because it is
the Word of the creative freedom of God. It did
not come to tell us we are free but to make
us free, and therefore to make our freedom dependent on its Maker's redeeming act. It is the
word of an absolute authority, whose holy love
alone has moral *power* to liberate the world. To
believe otherwise, or to believe anything short of
this, is to become more libertarian than evangelical,
to centre on man rather than on God, to be more
concerned for the freedom of the subject than the
freedom of the king. This may be sound politics
but is religious ruin ; it practically makes God to
be the servant of man's freedom more than man
the glory of God's. And to remain churches our
liberty must regain the primacy of love's holy,
authoritative, and sovereign note.

This is the line of progress, the line that Independency must take if it is to retain for the coming
age the sympathetic and divining power which
made it forward to meet the need of the aspiring age
now passing away. It must be even more sure and
ready with the note of authority than it was with

the note of liberty, with the authority that creates
spiritual liberty than with the liberty that creates
a social authority. It must be bound to its free
Gospel, and it must be more sure of the Gospel than
of the freedom, else its liberty becomes a cant.   If
it look to the Gospel God will see to the freedom.
If we seek first the freedom of His grace He will
see to our liberty of thought, speech, and action.
Can we offer the world an authority as real as
other churches and more free ?   The hour has come
when, for the sake of the world's true freedom,
the Church must convey first the authority of God,
and make it welcome and effective for faith and
conduct.   That is the first need of the time, and
it is also the first note of the Church.   And the
Church therefore is more happily situated than
when the world's first demand was but the freedom
which is the Church's second charge.   What is
entrusted to the Church is not simply redemption,
far less mere emancipation ; but it is redemption
by the Holy, and redemption into His holiness,
the redemption of society into that obedience in a
kingdom, and into the freedom that waits only
upon such obedience.

Has Independency anything in the nature of this
authority to offer the world ?   Is ours a *founded*
freedom ?   If not its day is done.   It cannot
mediate in industrial strife.   No church now can—

though it can teach in time of peace the principles that do mediate. But if it cannot mediate in the vast schism that both rends the soul in itself, and tears it from its true Lord and His obedience, it has no mission left. What it has to bring to Humanity is not a great asset but a great control, not man's ally but man's Lord and his God. It stands in the midst of the democracy, but it stands with God's Word to command the democracy quite as much as to rally it. Has it such a commanding creating Word ? If it have such a Word can it be anything but what I have said ? Not a Bible, not a Church, not a courage, nor a comfort, nor a stimulus, nor an ideal, but that—the Gospel of a God of holy love, with such right and such a redemption as leaves us not our own at all, and makes our total obedience our only pride.

I

MAY I gather up what has been said, even if I repeat while I reinforce? The early Independency, we have seen, rested on two large elements in general, and on certain factors of these in particular. In general it rested, first, on Calvinism, and, second, on that movement which, according to our taste, we shall call the cadet branch, the poor relation, or the camp-follower of the Reformation, described in a single term as Anabaptism. It did not draw directly from the Lutheran wing. Luther mortgaged Protestantism (under whatever necessity) when he dropped the Independency that at first seemed, even to himself, the direct corollary of his faith, and put his movement under the aegis of the princes of the day. Calvin offered much more support to a self-governing Church, and we have been used to think that Independency was born from Calvinism alone. That we have seen to be a mistake. It was when Calvinism was mingled

with what was best in the free spirit of Anabaptism,
now in England risen from its martyrdom and
purified of its socialism, that it founded the Independency which brought the Reformation to its
own in the public history of the world's freedom
and progress.

The Anabaptist element in Independency has
been discussed with some fulness. It is of immense
importance, and has been very singularly overlooked or scorned, even in Independency itself.
We may here only recall that its theological principle was one which to-day is the source of much
keen conflict and anxiety with us. It was the
Spirit, or the Christian consciousness, as something
co-equated with the Word ; co-equated and therefore entitled to be critical of it. Whereas it pro-
ceeds only from the Word—proceeding in such a
way that the Gospel is immune from any attack
by its own spirituality come of age, and is independent of any authority outside itself through its
experienced miracle of the new creation. If we
say that the theology of Modernism (Protestant
or Catholic) is a psychological theology of the
faith, and the theology of orthodoxy a historical
theology of the facts, and if we find neither of
these tenable alone, we may speak of a positive
theology of the fact within faith. It is historic in
that it turns on God's eternal act of salvation in

time, and psychological in that it has no religious meaning except as it enters and creates the new consciousness of the saved. What we really rally to is not the facts of the Bible or Church, but their central, creative, and therefore controlling fact— the Gospel in living power.

The Calvinistic element in Independency was in detail fourfold. It involved—

1. Predestination ;
2. An infallible Bible ;
3. A real sense of the Church, and the ecclesiastical finality of its first century form ;
4. Christ in His Word and Spirit.

1. Too much cannot be made of the predestination idea for the history of civil and religious freedom. It is but a young and amateur revolt that thinks the connection absurd. Modern democracy owes itself to Calvin. It had an Anabaptist mother, but he is its spiritual father. Beyond history it arose in the theology of the decrees of God. The soul's certainty of its direct predestination—that was what both created and controlled the personalism (sinking into the individualism) which has been the mainspring of modern democracy. From England the influence went to America ; and the foundation of the greatest republic the world ever saw rebounded upon France (though, alas, without

the control), and did more than even Rousseau to frame the ideas of its Revolution.

2. As to the infallible book, here again it is easy for the neophyte to make merry with such an idea to-day. But it is hard to see what could have taken the place of that idea when the infallible Church had fallen, and the faith of an infallible Gospel had not yet ascended to its place—as indeed it has not now.

3. With the infallible book was bound up, in those unhistorical days, the idea of the finality of the first century, especially as to Church order. We have learned differently, though our weakest point is still our historic sense. But at least the error carried with it what we rapidly lose—a real sense of the Church as the supernatural, and therefore the mightiest, society on earth.

4. And in respect of the old consciousness of the presence of Christ with such a Church in His redeeming Word and Spirit, there would be some variety of opinion to-day as to the sense in which the words should be taken, as will appear.

When we enumerated these (or other such) elements which went to the making of Independency we were not yet done. So great a world power could not be a mere compound of previously existing elements. It was not a mere amalgam, nor a mere product. In recent thought it is doubted if

any effect is but the exhibition of something that
was already in the cause, whether in every effect
there is not something original and peculiar to
itself.   And the dubious axiom is more than
doubtful when we are in the moral region of the
historical world.   In our present connection we
had to face the question why these elements, all
of which had long been at work abroad before
Independency became a power here, did not produce the same effect there ; why there has been
no Nonconformist Independency in the Protestantism of the Continent.   And we had therefore
to reckon in another and original factor, the special
contribution of the English genius for liberty and
self-government, which provided the one medium
in which all these Reformation elements could
combine fruitfully and firmly for the public and
progressive liberty of the world, both in its promotion and its control.

But now let us continue our inquiry as to what
our present position and prospects are in view of our
original constituents, on the one hand, and of our
public and historic service on the other.   Do we
preserve these constituents ?   If we do not, are we
therefore dispowered for continuing the work in
the world which they enabled our fathers to do ?
Theirs has been a tremendous work when we measure
it by the whole value of its fruit in civil and religious

liberty—a work which chiefly enables the Church
to claim the paternity of modern freedom. Does
it exhaust our vocation ? Is it our one work in
the world ? Were we raised up but for this, and,
having done it, should we regard it as enough for
any one section of the Church to have contributed
to Humanity ; and may we honourably retire, cultivate our own garden, and pass the great tasks
of the future to other hands ? Do we now linger
on, as Judaism has long and not ignobly done since
it produced the one Liberator of the Soul ? Where
we were once a world power, with effects indelible
and inexhaustible in history, are we now to be but
a little clan left with a great relic, a sect living on
great memories with little ways, saying small things
with a loud insignificant voice, and repeating
historic words as a class recites history ? Are we
going into dock only to be kept in good order and
great honour, as the *Victory* lies in Portsmouth
harbour, towed to her last berth—Nelson's deck
now left by Nelson's power ? Are we the pensioned remnant of a world conquest ?

To that question it might first be answered thus.
We might refer to the fact that even out of the
eighteenth century a second world conquest was
inaugurated by Independency, when its political
and social victory was well afloat and able to go
of itself. The Congregationalists and Baptists were

again the pioneers of a world idea which was waiting in the Church for a fit organ to give it hands and feet. More than a century ago they were the founders of modern missions, and of all that these have come to mean and to promise since then. Truly it needed but the lead, the one word to let loose the gathered waters, and the other churches were quickly on the field. I only wish to trace the persistency in Independency of a certain world-mission, an evangelical imperialism, its service to that side of Christianity which has charge of its ecumenical freedom and progress on a firm and permanent base of Gospel. The true ecumenical is the evangelical. I may also use the opportunity in passing to recall the fact that the plantations of the Commonwealth were missionary enterprises in Cromwell's intention. And, further, that the Pilgrim Fathers went out not only to seek their own freedom of worship, but to spread into savage lands (alas, at points in a too savage way !) the power of the Gospel. As it was said in a document of the time, they went ' from an inward zeal and great hope of laying some foundation, or making way for propagating the kingdom of Christ to the remote ends of the earth ; though they should be but stepping-stones to others.' The missionary passion, the passion for liberty, and the passion of the Gospel, all go together ; though

in practice one may outrun the rest for a particular age.

But a reference to our part in modern missions
is no sufficient answer to the question we have
raised. We may still be told that we have no
monopoly of missions, that the state of our missions
is somewhat unsatisfactory, and that, like other
churches, we do not rise to the opportunities we
once had power to create. Did our churches not
originate that enterprise under conditions which
have now disappeared ? In the changes of belief
and interest that have taken place have we parted
with the sources of our effective power both for
political and evangelical progress ?

Certainly the change is great, and we have
parted with much that made our fathers what
they were and determined what they did. Taking
the four elements I have enumerated we have
parted with the place of doctrine in life, and
especially with the doctrine of predestination as
Calvin had it. We have parted with the old position of the Bible, and certainly with the idea of an
infallible Bible as our fathers understood it, for
some better thing. We have parted with the
ecclesiastical finality of the New Testament age
and stage. We do not claim for Independency
divine right as being the polity consecrated and

embalmed for all time in the New Testament.
And we are tempted to part with a real sense of
a Church as distinct from any other association
for religious purposes. We do not draw a red
line between Church and World; membership
does not register a passage from death to life;
the Church has not a life as autonomous as that
of the world; and we are more prone to adopt the
methods of the world for the Church than to impose
the principles of the Church on the world. In
regard to the presence of Christ with the Church
in His Word and Spirit, there are signs that this
is, for certain churches, a piece of their theology
rather than the principle of their practice. The
relation between the historic Christ and His Spirit
is often far from clear. The Church of the Spirit
claims the right, in many places, to sit in judgment
on the Christ of the Word. And the Anabaptist
detachment and co-equation of Word and Spirit
is the active principle in many who take the
matter so slightly that they may complain that
they do not know what the phrase means.

The question, therefore, is this—If these doctrines
or principles made and inspired the Independency
in whose creative place for the modern world we
take our pride, do they make also its continuity;
and can Independency continue to thrive with
like aim or a like effect without them ? It is a

twofold question. Can Independency go on to live without positive doctrine in prominent place ? Can any church form a real unity except on the basis of what it believes in common ? Can a subjective sympathy unite a church as a common object of faith does ? And, if Independency is bound up with positive Christian doctrine, does it rest upon any doctrine or principle which is not equally represented by other churches which have perhaps better machinery for giving it effect ?

If we attempt to answer that question in either form we must fall back on the fourth factor of those I named, and take stand on the saving and ruling presence of Christ with us in His Word and Spirit ; and on that as understood in a special way which has our large old Independent outlook, but turns it on the future rather than the past.

There is no doubt that the great world problem for the future of the reformed churches is their union. The union of the churches and the conditions that realise it make a far more urgent task for us at the moment than the direct conquest of the world's opposition, whether rational or practical, whether its criticism or its paganism. We shall never master the world, either apologetically or evangelically or socially we can never take the terror of life from the poor, till the churches are

welded, with whatever relative independency, round
some one central point which is the source of our
solidary power, spiritual freedom, and ample hope.
The Church's liberality of thought, or comprehension, or beneficence, must flow from its generosity of
new life, from the greatness of its Gospel, and not
from the range of the ideas we can associate with
it. This union is the new form of the old problem
so finely and eagerly pressed by Richard Baxter
before its time, the old idea for which Cromwell
so greatly stood in politics, in his liberal, sound,
but also premature, principle of toleration for all
Christians (to say nothing of Jews and Turks),
so long as they did not, like the Catholics,
plot against the State. The political tolerance of
Cromwell took more intimate shape in Baxter as
ecclesiastical comprehension ; but both were on a
fixed base, and were held impossible otherwise.
Such men were very clear as to what was meant
by a Christian. They said he was a man who,
whatever views he might hold on other points,
trusted to the soul-blood of Christ for the forgiveness of his sins and eternal life.   With his powerful
practical insight Cromwell seized on the very
immortal soul of his Independency when he found
the marrow of true Christianity here : ' Those who
believe the remission of sins through the blood of
Christ, and free justification through the blood of

U

Christ; who live upon the grace of God; those men who are certain they be so—they are members of Jesus Christ.'—*Lett.*, ii. 444.

The greatest problem before Independency is how to regain its place in the great world Church; and to do it, not by the ineffective way of mere sympathy, which may begin and end in sentiment, but by some way which shall make the Church a real and respected power for the practical purpose of God with society. And that we shall never do simply in the name of a Christian charity, nor in that of a Christian liberty, which alone will but make us a refuge of cranks; but only in the name of the only Authority which creates a liberty we can never force.

Now it is from this point of view that we must construe that position which I named as outlasting all the other factors that made us, and as carrying us on into the future with the word of reconciliation for the sects—' the real and ruling presence of Christ in His Word and Spirit.' Only we must give to the *Word* a new sense which is the soul of the old. By the Word we do not mean the Bible, we mean the redeeming Gospel which put the Bible there. And by the Spirit we mean more than a power of warm light which illuminates the book it falls on; we mean a power which issues from the altar whose cathedral the book is, and turns the living gospel Word into living and personal experience.

The historic and ultimate fact is not the Bible. The Bible, and the Bible alone, is not the religion of Protestants.   Nor is it Christ in the sense of the mere phenomenon of Christ's historic personality acting impressively upon us from afar—what might be called the personalism of Jesus.   But it is Christ construed in a certain way, as doing with His whole personality a certain unique and timeless thing.   It is not the history of Jesus, but the Act of God and God's grace in the history of Jesus. It is Christ's person as interpreted by the New Testament, the whole New Testament Christ, and not merely what has been lightly called the Christ of the gospels.   For the Christ of the gospels was a supplementary presentation of Him to churches that had been made by the gospel that fills the Epistles.   It is the Christ of the apostles, Christ as self-interpreted in the apostles, Christ not simply as the perfectly divine soul, but as charged with an eternal work He had to finish, Christ as the eternal redeeming Son of God, perfect not in spiritual aspect but in moral vocation, not as character but as Redeemer.   It is the whole Christ crucified, Christ with His whole historic person pointed in the Cross, Christ positivised in the Word of the Gospel, and am-

plified and glorified in the Spirit. It is the Lord
the Spirit—the Spirit not co-equated with the
Son, as if He were an independent and even
corrective power, but the Spirit as coming from
the Father through the work of the Son, the
Spirit inseparable for saving purposes, and for
the Church's life, from the Word of the Gospel,
ordering and correcting all things from there,
but correcting that and superseding that never.
This means, of course, a repudiation of that side
of our Anabaptist descent which made the Spirit
another and higher dispensation than the Son.

In a word, the hope of the union of the reformed
churches is in no tradition of line or succession, but
in the spiritual succession alone; not by apostolical
succession, but by evangelical solidarity; not as
sons of Abraham, but as sons of the promise. *This
means a church of one article.* It is the Gospel of
grace and of faith in the salvation which is in Jesus
Christ, the Gospel not of personality but of personality redemptive and redeemed. The centrality
and sufficiency of such a gospel is the one condition
of church unity. And for this church of one
article we have a legacy of facilities which the
other churches have not; we have a mobility on
that authoritative base which is not theirs, and
which appeals to the swiftness of the democratic
time. We are the flying squadron, the advance

guard, the democratic side of the super-democratic Church. This is our *metier*; not freedom of thought, not theological freedom. Pure theology has fortunately never been our goal, as I have pointed out. We do not exist for pure doctrine. But we have been set, in our English way, for the quick translation of a fundamental theology, a theological gospel, into ethical and social life.

It is not the only service to the kingdom. Other churches other lots and other tasks. The churches are complementary. But it is a great and urgent service of the pioneer sort which has always been our ideal—often misleading us, but always keeping our faces to Jerusalem, sometimes inflating us, sometimes shooting up without deepness of earth, but on the whole making us the pathfinders of the public hour. Not indeed (as I have said) the pioneers of theological development. The development of doctrine is not the chief part of the work given us to do. It was not the work given to the English Reformation, which came in Independency to its true head and effect. We were delivered in great measure from that resurgence of scholasticism which made Lutheran orthodoxy in the seventeenth and eighteenth century a new Egypt for the new Israel. We were not supremely concerned with the determination of dogma, or the culture of pure doctrine ; it was with the religious, social, and political application of dogma (and of one dogma in particular, the most mighty of all for personal faith—predestination). We were called for its application as the fundamental principle of religious and social life, for the constitution of the Church by it, and then for the moulding of all social life on the principle of that eternal society. We were not, as a people, or as a section of the Church, concerned with school questions, but with questions of life, public and private, on everlasting foundations. In our day we were the Christian trustees of public progress by popular power, and the stewards of the true social genius of the Reformation, whereby Protestantism has become that blessing to the modern world which the Roman Church was to the world of the middle age. It was, I repeat, the right we asserted for every local church freely to determine and conduct its affairs that became the foundation of the public principle so great and beneficent for the modern world—the sovereignty of the people.

Upon English soil alone were the two great movements of the Reformation age adjusted and consummated—Reformers and Anabaptists; the Evangelical and the Libertarian; the Word and the Spirit; Fixity and Freedom; Faith and Inspiration; Reformation and Renovation; and it was in Independency that this most fruitful union took place. Such is our hereditary genius—not liberty alone, but the combination of positivity and liberty, of authority and progress, of security and freedom; wherein the liberty is secured by the positivity, being the freedom that flows from a given and historic Christ for every interest of mankind. We represent a free soul-faith on the base of a historic authority, with an incorrigible bias to public affairs, and the resolve to secure the establishment of the Church in the only real way—its establishment not by law but in the laws, not as a church favoured by national preference, but as the Church's Christianity glorified in national conduct.

I will approach the same matter from another side, and still from history. The Toleration Act of 1689 gave up the principle which had ruled the English Church from Henry viii. to James ii.—the principle of the essential unity of Church and State, which had taken its last expression in the Act of Uniformity in 1662. With 1689 came a principle totally different (though for long afterwards, and even to this day, very imperfectly realised in fact) —liberty of religious conviction so far as the State is concerned, the State's neutral recognition of a variety of religious communities on the foundation of the Reformation gospel. Nonconformity had been penal and without rights ; it now received status, subject to a recognition of the existing government and obedience to the law. That is to say, the Puritan and Independent element, which hitherto had been *within* the State Church, now became a *body* of Dissent *alongside* that Church, to grow later into an *army against* the Church in so far as established. The great battle which had been the supreme interest of English history for a century and a half, the central conflict of the national life, had been an ecclesiastical conflict. It is inadequate to see in the long campaign but the struggles of nationalism, or even industrialism, or the slow upheaval of *couches sociales*. If it is not theology that has been the supreme issue of English history, it has been the practical application of theology. Can any one with such a commanding view-point believe that that warfare is now but among forgotten far-off things ? But there was then ended one great stage of it— nay, the greatest. The principle at least was settled. That stage was the battle between Episcopacy and Puritanism, Institution and Faith. And Puritanism, through Independency, had won. The principle of public liberty in Christ's Gospel, which had become the historic trust and task of Independency in English history, was now substantially established—though not completely. And a great

epoch was closed in the history of England and of
Protestantism. The Stuarts had staked the king on
the bishop and were checkmated. They identified
the fate of throne and Church. And with the
Church went down the throne. It was the Lord's
doing. For it was the Gospel that won against the
Church. This was the real English Reformation—
this, and not Henry's, and not Elizabeth's. The
German Reformation was not a final but a progressive thing ; and it was in England that it ran
its native course. The Gospel won permanently
against the Church, which had ceased to be its
steward ; and it won by means of the sects. It
was by means of the sects, with all their extravagances, that this solid and permanent conquest
came. But with the winning of this victory they
subsided to become more sects than they were
before—less extreme, perhaps, but more of sects.

I mean it in this sense. They ceased now to
have the old significance for the history of the great
Church, or of collective Protestantism. They had
still much work to do in consolidating their own
free existence. (Much, alas ! they did also in disintegrating and rending it.) They had an even
vaster work to do by following up their victory in
the region of political liberty, and in preparing a
religious habitation for the new democracy, both in
its commercialist and its industrialist stage. They

developed a vigorous denominational life, and a valuable type of piety and vital godliness. But they were more universal for the State than the Church. They ceased to be an influence on the course of the world-Church. In this direction their productive power was spent. They have not, for instance, been productive in the region of theology, in the development of Protestant truth and its adjustment to the new intellectual age. They have been even appropriative in this respect but slowly. They contributed much to the detachment of English Christianity from continental, and its insular seclusion from wider influences. And they have largely lost the historic spirit and sense of continuous tradition, lost it in voluntary associations, *a priori* views, and immediate experiences. They do not affect the constitution of the more historic churches [*see* note at the end of the chapter], though they rear great young communions beside them. Nor do they now affect the political constitution in the same thorough way as in the Revolution of 1688. For though we have just seen the greatest change since then, and one in which the Nonconformists have been playing a great part, yet it is not directly as Nonconformists. The central issue with the House of Lords recently was not ecclesiastical as it was in 1688. The spearhead of the Liberal movement

for the hour is not Nonconformity though it may
be its backbone. And the driving power is a
social rather than a religious interest—one, indeed,
which often professes to despise the churches.
Its leadership has passed from the churches to
influences that have a loose, or even a negative,
connection with them.

The churches tended, especially in the eighteenth
century, to draw into themselves and become
closed circles, with beliefs to correspond. The
elaborate Calvinism of many of our trust-deeds
is a deposit of that century, when they became
free and secure enough to build ; and it is a record
of that scholastic debasement to orthodoxy which
is apt to mark an age which has come spent out
of a great conquest. If the Restoration was
a vehement reaction against Puritan ethic, the
orthodoxy of the eighteenth century was in extravagant reaction from the Anabaptist extravagance of the sectaries with whom Cromwell
had to part. It is the same phenomenon that
meets us in the early centuries of Christianity
itself ; and the same fate that fell on the Reformation in Germany in the seventeenth century.
The divisions I have named were a result of
this temper, this tendency to coagulate through
standing unstirred by the greater issues of a
Church. The Calvinism of that age is not the

molten thought of the great age. It is Calvinism clotted, and sometimes soured. Many of the members of the churches, moreover, passed to Unitarianism (through Arianism) in one direction, and into Methodism in the other. Independency, however, was perhaps less affected in this fissiparous way than any other body, owing to its tradition of liberty upon a fixity which was central and not peripheral, fundamental and not circumstantial, evangelical rather than theological.

II

Dissent has thus become sectarian in respect of its contribution to the great historic Church and its unity. But sectarian with a difference—sectarian as Christianity was to the Judaism in which it rose, and not sectarian like the mystic groups of the Middle Ages. It was composed of sects that were growing into churches, and slowly preparing once more to take their place in the federal unity of that great Church to which alone is promised the conquest of the world for the kingdom of God. The idea of the Church which prevails over the greater part of the world is that of an institution whose security rests upon the integrity of a long historic tradition, an unbroken succession and a visible organisation. That idea has to be altered, and altered for the better. Another conception of the Church must be made the dominant in the world's mind. The Church must be re-defined, in the thought even of a world that stands outside it; and not as an institution, but as the society of the evangelical succession and the regenerative power. And this is a work that can only be begun by the union, the federation (not the amalgamation) of all the churches that stand on an evangelical instead of an institutional foundation on the one hand, or a subjective or rational foundation on the other. It must be done by the federate, and what has been called the charitative, action of all such reformed churches in mutual respect, confidence, and affection. This is the Church problem of the future for them.

Has the Independent tradition, then, any special part to play, any special contribution to make to this end? Others of the free churches have been doing their share in cementing their past divisions, and dressing their line before the enemy. The Baptists have done so, the Methodists have. Independency has not been split into these divisions; what then is prescribed by history for it? What tradition has it still to make good in the new situation?

Up till now, to a large extent, its work has been too negative—a very great and most necessary work, but negative after all. It has been a struggle for liberty. But mere liberty is a negative idea apart from a creative authority. And we have been doing more for liberty than for authority—with the result now of a dangerous crisis. For in a Church of the Gospel the authority that sets free must always be prior to the freedom it makes.

I said the great battle of English history was a Church conflict. It was to detach State and Church into the true freedom, and therefore the true power, of each. The principle of that separation we established in the Revolution Settlement. But the principle made slow way in detailed practice. It is still a long way from complete realisation. And ever since 1688 the Independents have been in the van of those who pursued the great national and spiritual mission of securing its effects in the Church's release from the State. But it is, after all, the negative side of the whole work. Disestablishment is but ending a wrong relation of the Church to the State; we have yet to establish the right relation. It is folly to think and live as if there were no relation. Our positive task is to establish in our country a spiritually free Church, were it but for the sake of the freedom of the State. But it is far more for the sake of a free faith, which again is there only for the sake of a free grace.

Now the negative part of this work—Disestablishment—has passed, or is passing, out of our hands. It has become an essential question of practical politics, the politics of a whole composite party, largely, of course, made up of ourselves in our civic capacity. We have committed it to the hands of faithful men, who will see that it come to pass in the interests of civil liberty and public equality. This is another of those interests or tasks which, like education, or the care of the poor, were created and reared by the Church, but are now passed over to the charge of society, as a prime interest of its own.[1]

But the other, the positive, side, the establishment in the heart and affairs of society of a church

---

[1] The like applies to liberal thought. That passes to the care of the State Universities. Even in theology this is so. There ought to be facilities for the cultivation of thought and knowledge absolutely free in religious matters. And it is in a university that these should exist. They cannot in a church. For a church is there for a free gospel, and not for free research. The word 'free' does not mean the same thing in each case. The Church has a gospel in first trust which limits the intellectual freedom within it to what does not destroy that gospel. The university can have no such limitation. For the Church the gospel is final, for the schools nothing can be final. The one aims at a free soul, the other at free thought. The Church may and must accept the results of free thought, but only up to the point when they destroy a free gospel. The final must then send the non-final back for revision and more experience—especially more experience of the religious experience itself. Free thought lies as a first charge, therefore, not on the Church but on the university ; and those churches, which have been cherishing it as a special trust, and which think the Church should not be behind the schools in this kind of freedom, must come to see that it is not the freedom for which a Church exists, but that it must be counted among the things that, through its universities, a State can do better, because it is its proper work.

free for the service of Christ, for free grace and the
final kingdom—that is now borne in upon us with
an urgency that balances this release on the negative side. The less we need to be a protesting
church, so much the more we must realise a
catholic church; and the more must we present
the true catholicity to the world, and on that
base the true unity. What special service, then,
is Independency in a position to render to this
task of the future, this task of converting the
world's idea of Catholicism from the hierarchical
to the evangelical (even while rescuing it from
many evangelicals) ? Something is very specially
incumbent on Independency here. It was the
chief influence in calling the modern democracy
into being ; it is debtor to correspond in the
matter of its guidance. Now Independency alone
cannot guide the democracy. For one thing, it
is in practice too dependent on it. But indeed
no mere section of the Church can be such a
guide to a whole phase of civilisation—only the
Church as a whole can, and the Church as the
apostle of a final and authoritative gospel which
is universal in its permeating as well as its co-
ordinating power. Only a united Church has the
promise to control that whole democracy which
a sectional Church had the commission to create.
And only a Church can which is the apostle of the

gospel of man's new unity in Christ. That is
the only true apostolic succession—the creative
legacy of Gospel power and of the Holy Ghost.
The Gospel of Christ in a united Church is the
only influence that can mould the fierce democracy to the kingdom of God. Of course if
the democracy has other ideals than the kingdom
of God it will seek other means than the Gospel
of realising them. But that is our positive power.
Our idealism has served and impelled us well—till
it become our sole religion. But then it breaks
down. For the constant tendency of idealism,
especially in a minority and in opposition, is
that it becomes too exclusively negative and
critical. It then carps, rasps, and bites. In the
history of thought, to say nothing of politics,
mere idealism becomes but critical idealism. It
is not constructive. It is to the front only at
question time, and it is apt to become a source
of more diversion than effect. This will always be
the weakness of mere idealism, either in thought
or affairs. It cannot create. It cannot create
or sustain a social body to be its engine. It
falls into cultured groups, sets, or intellectual
fashions. It becomes a cult of culture—at its
moral best, of personality, at its worst, of fads.
It is not a gospel, and therefore it cannot make
a church. Such is the criticism of clear-eyed

x

idealists on their own idealism; and they feel the enormous, the infinite, advantage possessed by even an impossible orthodoxy in its power to make and carry on a church because it has a gospel. We are neither orthodoxists nor mere idealists. We are Gospellers. We are Churchmen. We believe in the churches, in the Church. Well, what special service can we render in turning the churches into the Church, in enabling the churches to do for the public what the Church alone can do, not in erasing the churches by a church, but in federating them into the Church ?

The question, therefore, which becomes for us of first importance is the positive one. And it concerns not only our contribution to personal religion, or to social welfare, but to the whole Church in the whole world. Now the Church is a historic body; it is not simply an accidental and voluntary body in the sense of being whatever any group or age may choose to make it, without reference either to theological reality or historic tradition. To answer our question positively, therefore, means that we ask what the problem is which is set up by the history we inherit— European and national. Every great movement (like the Reformation) has been great not simply because it preached a certain idea, but because it

put it in the terms of the question as history had
raised it, and answered that question.   It was to
the great medieval question that Luther gave an
answer so great.   Now it has been pointed out
already that the political genius of our English
history and constitution has taken the form of
an ecclesiastical conflict.   Our stable and model
liberty has arisen from a prolonged struggle
between State and Church.   But it would be a
shallow mistake to treat the struggle simply as
a long effort on the part of the State to shake
off the Church, or of the Church to settle on
the neck of the State.   Such a view savours too
much of village, platform, or press polemic.   The
classic period of the conflict was from Henry VIII.
to William III.   The two powers to it were Church
and State.   And there were two ideas as to their
relation.   One was represented by Episcopacy and
its establishment.   It bound a certain form of
Church polity in the closest way with the polity,
policy, and institutions of the nation ; and it
gave the Church, by its national place and power,
a place and influence also in the great history
of the West.   It continued the medieval intimacy
of the Church with great affairs, and it did so
in a way more successful than any arrangement
the Middle Ages reached abroad.   The other of
these ideas was represented by Puritanism, ending

in Nonconformity. It took its start not from the idea of the nation, nor even from a corporate church, but from the inwardness, spirituality, and freedom of the redeemed soul. Its social unit was a community, not an institution. Its church was the community of the saints. It was thus that it strove to carry out the Reformation principle, and realise the idea of the Church unseen. Its whole contention came to turn on the autonomy and value of the local community. Its problems were not theological so much as practical. Independency erased the distinction between the theologian and the layman more completely than any other. No church was so little a church of its ministers, influential as these were. It was influence that they had, and not power. The priesthood of all believers here first became practical and effective for church life. It created the reality of Christian freedom by the divine place it secured for the Christian individuality. A man became a man because he was his own priest in Jesus Christ. The voluntary principle became the whole principle of English Nonconformity. Truly it frayed out on its edges to mere atomism and petty schism; but what a value it has had for personal piety, for practical Christianity, and especially for the infusion of Christian ethic into political life.

These were the two ideas that struggled with

each other to regulate the relation of Church and State. Which of them gives more promise of power to christianise the State, or the national conduct at least ? Neither, perhaps, can look for absolute victory in what of the battle is yet to come. Each represents an element essential to the whole case. I have already said that we cannot simply sever Church and State and leave them lying apart. We cannot proceed as if there were no relation between them. We cannot cleave the soul in that way, especially when it is occupied with its greatest interests, and most especially with its supreme interest in the unity of God. The unity of the soul itself, and therefore of the Christian life, prescribes some form of unity, of polarity, between Church and State. Simple and absolute severance is too summary, too abstract, and too negative. We all feel that more or less. Some of the extremest separatists are also among those who would most directly and impatiently apply the principles, and even the pressure, of the Christian Church to political society, and especially to political action. And so alongside of the strife of the two ideas in our history there has from time to time appeared a third, which took the shape of some effort at union among the reformed churches for the purpose of bringing the pure and powerful influences of an inward

Christianity to bear upon national life and affairs. Such was Baxter's effort, wonderfully welcome but not finally successful; or the movement which preceded the Savoy conference. Had they succeeded, we might have seen the finest triumph of Protestantism—some arrangement which should do justice both to the long tradition of the Church's constitution, and also to the reformed freedom of the single community and of the spiritual soul. The attempt was doomed to failure at that day. The fatal involution of the Episcopate with the monarchy arrested it on the one side ; and, on the other, the Reformation principles were not yet clearly adjusted—the true relation between history and the soul, between the Word and the Spirit, between the Bible and the Christian conscience, between the formal and the material principle of Protestantism. Each side was still too extreme. And within Protestantism itself, within Independency, there was that isolation and over-pressing of the Christian consciousness, that exaggeration of the material principle of subjective faith, that dream of being free by casting loose from all historic and objective authority, even in Scripture—a liberty unmoored and uncharted, a freedom which gnaws out its own interior, and leaves it the prey of unrest without object and of action without end.

Baxter's problem is in abeyance, but it is not solved. Our negative success has not yet made us quite realise our positive task for the public, or take ourselves in hand most earnestly for its achievement. The Church must be a power with the State. How ? For it is the only organ of Christianity when we come to action upon our national society, as, indeed, upon human society altogether. The glance we have just cast upon our history may indicate the nature of this positivity, so desirable, so necessary.

We may let ourselves be reminded that when Independency conquered it was not its programme that prevailed, nor its policy, it was its principle. The Commonwealth went down ; and Congregationalism has not become the one form of free church life. It was the idea, the genius, of Independency that survived, that has secured so much liberty for the congregation even in churches closely connectional, that has worked in the world quite apart from our churches, and has gained the greatest of modern victories in the supreme sovereignty of the people.

How is it with the other power—the Episcopal Church taken as the National ? Is it otherwise ? Is there not an idea, a genius, a principle there ? Have we not just been obliged to own it ? Have we not seen that it is impossible for a church like the Christian to be absolutely out of relation to the national life and its public conduct ; that a society so great, living, and ethical as the Church must have a close and powerful influence of a practical kind on the great life of politics and the State ; that its principles ought to become the ethical principles of a State which rises in the moral scale ; that the Christian principle in trust of the Church should control public behaviour, if not in the same form, yet as surely as with private life ?   That, or something like that, is the inner principle of establishment behind its empirical form.   The State is not pagan.   It is not material.   It has a soul.   And it ought to have a Christian soul.   And it ought to express it—if not in worship or privilege, yet in public law, conduct, and history.   Individualism, conventiclism, sectarianism, do not represent the due position of Christianity in State or nation, nor its due respect from either.   They do not give effect to the Christian kingdom of God.   If all members of the State were Christians by conversion, as the old Church continues to hold they are by baptism, then there would be, by their moral Gospel, a very vital and urgent relation between the Church of their conversion and the State of their affairs.   That is the permanent idea of the Established Church, amid all its obvious failure to make the nation really Christian, all the injustice

of its actual position; this is the idea permanent
amid all the change that has been, or may be, in
the form that establishment takes—the close and
powerful connection of Christianity, through the
Church, with the national life and its greatest
expressions in act. Our denationalisation has cost
us so much that it has left us without power to
realise how much.

And that effective influence is what the free
churches must somehow ensure under the conditions of spirituality, equality, and autonomy.
The Church as free must do what the Church
as established has failed to do for this idea. It
must do more to christianise the State and its
politics, civil and foreign. And it cannot do this
except by its own internal union. The State, the
nation, will not be christianised towards God's
Kingdom by competitive sects, but only by a
federate Church of one Gospel for one Humanity.
And there is no foundation, no secret, for this
union but that we should repair, with a new
straitness, intensity, and power, to the central
Gospel which gives us our right to be, and to
be free; that we should neglect everything else
in comparison with the confession and declaration of that gospel, in such forms of expression,
practical or theological, as may be prescribed by
the forces and necessities of the time ; and that

our unity must lie in our confession of the mighty truth in our charge before it can take any effect as co-operation in the good works waiting to be done.

Our great positive task, therefore, is not social reform, political pressure, or philanthropic energy, but something which empowers and fertilises all these. It is not even evangelisation, in the current sense of the word. It is effective union of the federal, and not the imperial, kind, of the devolutionary kind, and not the centralised; convergent only on the common, but moralised, gospel of churches which are complementary in their action under that centripetal faith. It is only on such union that we can base a united moral effect on the world.

This is a matter so great and vital to us and to society that it is worth while to dwell on it, and turn it round at fresh angles. What is the modern affair that lies nearest to the concern of any church ? What at the moment is the supreme interest of the Church within the world ? What is the greatest gift it can give the world ? What is its prime condition for reaching the world ? It is its own union. And how is such a union of the Church to come to pass ? Not by reorganisation of machinery, and not by combination for humane or ethical effect, but by renovation in the spirit of its mind and the quality of its Gospel. 'Say not ye,

A confederacy, a confederacy. The Lord of
Hosts Him shall ye sanctify,' as He has revealed
Himself in His saving will for a moral world.
The union which is the one thing needful at the
hour, the one pressing thing the Church owes
the world, can only grow from its concentration,
on its creative base, on the one positive Gospel
which makes a Church a Church ; and this even
to the comparative neglect for the hour, if need
be, of all that is but circumference to that.
When Baxter moved for union, the distinction
was introduced, which has since played so great
a part among us, between fundamentals and
circumstantials. And his fundamental, Presbyterian as he was, was the fundamental professed
by Independency alone, as expressed in Milton,
Cromwell, and even the sects. It was no theme of
scholastic theology, and no fabric of speculative
dogmatic. It was ethical, spiritual, experimental.
' Not the head makes the Christian, they said, but
the heart '—meaning thereby not the affectionate
nature, nor a promiscuous charity, but the heart
stablished by grace upon man's moral reconciliation
to God by the death of Jesus Christ. They stood
not upon the natural affections turned on God,
but upon the 'gracious affections' of the new
creation. This was the rock both of the soul
and of the Church. To this all else was circum-

stantial.   For this all else was free.   All sects which thus held the head should be tolerated by the State and recognised by each other.   Within that, ' difference in religion should not be a different religion,' as Burroughs said in his *Irenicum*.   Within that, differences did not represent different lines, but different angles of vision.   Whoever was there had, by that confession, an equal right and place with every other in the Church of Christ.   The free conscience among men, man's central and active freedom from men, was secured on the foundation of a conscience free by Christ with God.   We were never free without the absolute authority of a redeeming Christ.   With this all was free, and from this all else would flow.   " Necessary doctrines are not at all hard, nor require long time to learn.   For the Word of God having once planted this truth in the understanding, viz. that it is the blood of God which cleanseth us from all sins—this evangelical truth of its own nature would instantly set man on work to do the will of Him that so loved him."   So speaks a writing of the period.   It is the rediscovery of the fundamental principle of the Reformation, as so familiarly put by Melanchthon, but never before practically realised by the Reformers.   Independency was the first section of the Church deliberately to take this for the principle of Church union, and to found stability and liberty, first for Church and then for State, on one article which is the heart and spring of all else. Men, they said, may ruin themselves, this truth they could never ruin. They strove always to get back to the centre, to refer all the doctrines that made the sects to one trunk principle, which should be the fundamental statement of Christianity, and would give an equal right and protection to all who owned it in whatever variety. They found it in the reconciliation of man effected by God in the atoning death of Christ. And this practical faith became their one criterion of the Christianity either of a soul or a church, and the source of their liberty, first ecclesiastical and then political. Our very national, our political liberty was made by these men, and it thus has at last nothing but an evangelical base.

Have we no duty to this tradition ? Have we none of this legacy left to invest in modern affairs ? Have we nothing but the echo of barren and negative freedom ? Have we not rather a hereditary leadership of a positive kind in the direction in which the churches should most urgently go ? The leadership the religious age requires is not in the matter of liberty. That victory is practically won. It is in the matter of a rallying and creative authority. Have we any power to lead in this

new need and demand of the age ? Has Independency nothing in its tradition which commends
and commits it to the forward service of an age
whose demand has so changed ? Are we taken
quite aback and found resourceless by the new
requirement of the modern world ? Have we
nothing but the old tune of liberty to grind out
in the market-place, like blind men who play the
songs of boyhood, and cannot read any more the
quest in the faces of those who hurry by ? Has
this liberty become itself the modern orthodoxy,
which enslaves us to its dry jangle of traditional
phrase ? Have we become mere ἐλευθερόδουλοι,
slaves of liberty, and echoes of originality ?
Have we no power or liberty to tell the world
above all else what we are free for, or how we
are free ? Are we only free to stand aside from
the churches that can do so, and talk hypocriti-
cally of their bondage ? Can the liberty of Independency to-day do nothing to lead in pressing
upon all the Protestant Churches the uniting idea
of a federate Church of one living article, declaratory and not exclusory, whose experience gives the
Church at once its rock and its range, its ground
and its freedom ; one article which clearly tells
both its own catechumens and a world in arms
what the Church is ; one article which has in it the
inspiration of the Church's service, the condition

of its co-operation, the secret of its security, and
on whose base its liberty also should be established and protected from attacks either upon its
exercise or its honour. The Church of the future
must guarantee these two things, *security and
liberty*, and establish them for the moral and
spiritual soul. There is nothing which society at
large so much needs as these two things, one growing
from the other, which are the very being of the
Christian society. Will the Church never show
the world that it has the power of liberty without
breaking away into sects, or the power of security
without hardening up into dogma ? Has it no
liberty but what dissolves its own base, and no
security but what petrifies its liberty ? As one
Church, has it one truth, which is both its revelation and its inspiration, its law and impulse in one,
one Gospel which, like God Himself in making
man, gives the Church its freedom by the act of its
creation ? Is there any section of the Church
whose tradition points that way to the extent that
Independency does ? Has it not a hereditary duty
of such hegemony. It is not a question whether
Independency should do this for its own sake.
The times have advanced beyond a point of view
so sectarian. The question is removed and lifted
to the range of all the free churches and their
union. That union can only be on the base of an

explicit gospel. Is it not our traditional right, not, indeed, to reign over our brethren, far less to boast, but to carry the standard in their great procession, and renew to the world the testimony of our classic age, the witness of wide comprehension on the foundation of a positive gospel which is not a legal creed, but a worshipping confession. Other churches may have facilities for other things, such as social experiments, and organic enterprise. Have we not the tradition and secret of *founded freedom* ? Has Independency, in both its branches, not an ancestral aptitude and a historic commission to invite the sister churches of the reformed faith to rally into one federate Church of this Gospel, so simple, profound, and intimate, so free from bondage because so bound to the cross of our redemption, so hospitable to the higher criticism because so secured by grace in the great judgment, so ripe with social blessing because so brotherly in a world reconciliation ?

A very great effect was produced upon the world, and especially upon Anglicanism, by the publication of the Free Church Catechism, with its revelation of a massive and common belief. Still greater would be the effect of such a declaration in one article by all the free churches as their term of corporate communion. It could be declaratory only, to characterise and not delimit, for description and not for subscription, for confession and not for exclusion, with moral and not legal value, a covenant for the churches and a badge for their teachers rather than a test for their members, a reflection of the one Word which alone makes the one Church.

There is another point of view. The aspect of Church freedom which appeals most to a modern and cultured world is not so much the freedom of the Church from the State, as its freedom from its own past, freedom from orthodoxy, or from what is called external authority. Freedom of thought weighs more even than freedom of soul with a public which grows intelligent faster than it grows religious. It is an inevitable stage in the growth of a society which has just begun to taste education in large numbers, who are readily but vaguely impressed by academic, intellectualist, and æsthetic ideas. For free thought is a piece of the same intellectualism as is shown in orthodoxy, only that the one is moving, the other stationary. But however that be, there are many who are willing to put up with the drawbacks of a State Church, and do not trouble about its principle, because they think that it guarantees freedom of thought in theological matters, and secures a type of religion to correspond—genial, cultured, and inexigent. And there are those among ourselves who are not willing to be outdone by any church in such comprehension. But such a conception of freedom is entirely different from the idea of it that lies at the root of the free-church case. It should be made clear that free thought, if a real, is yet a secondary and sequacious interest from the free-church point of view. It has already been shown that the free churches, as they were born in England, are redolent of that moral and practical soil. They did not arise either in the theology or in the philosophy of the schools. They do not savour of academic liberty. They do not cultivate liberty for academic completeness but for evangelical fulness, for the freed conscience, for practical experience and action. Neither theology nor philosophy is, in itself, an English interest, and it was the English genius that went into the free churches. They are intensely national in their spiritual features, especially as regards local and individual liberty in Christ. They arose out of the interest of practical life—the life of the local church on the one hand and the experient soul on the other. They arose in the interest of the soul's liberty with God, and not the mind's liberty in the world, the interest of moral and evangelical liberty, not of intellectual, except as that is promoted and demanded by the other, and as a soul set free in God is free to range and realise His creation. Their congenial freedom is therefore freedom of

faith rather than of thought. They rest on that
freedom in God and His righteousness to which
all other freedom is duly added.

But we may stop to urge here that it *is* added.
Man's first concern is that God should be free, his
second is that he should be free before God ; it is
only thus, in the third place, that the freedom of his
thought becomes a concern ; whether its freedom
from past thought or its freedom from its neighbour's. But then it does become an inevitable concern, as part of the freedom of his confession of God's
liberty and God's redemption, whether in worship or
in thought. It is part of his duty and service to the
God of liberty and truth. It is a concern, therefore,
with a double foundation. Our freedom of thought
or worship rests on two pillars. First, it rests on
an evangelical basis—on God's free will of grace
in His revelation of Himself by His liberating
Gospel. And, second, it rests on a historic basis,
on the mental evolution which has been already
traversed in the Church as the field of that gospel's
expanding truth. We must continue the great
enlarging tradition of Christian thought — the
greatest in the world. This means that the truth
of the past is an essential condition, and even
an ingredient, in the truth of the present; and
that orthodoxy is rationally treated not when it is
dissolved and rejected, but only when it is understood, interpreted, and developed.

But our chief concern is with the former base, that of ultimate truth in God's final revelation of Himself, where not only our last reality comes by our Liberator, but He is Himself our only freedom. If we have not the warrant of our religious freedom there, we have it nowhere. As churches we are entitled only to such freedom as that inspires, demands, or implies. With the instinct of natural freedom we are not directly concerned. That is a matter of civil or academic interest. But our freedom of Christian thought is included. And I am anxious to point out the service that would be rendered to freedom of view and fulness of thought when the Church is clear and explicit about the one article of its positive and liberating gospel. Thought in the Church is hampered, first, for want of a single dynamic centre which does for the race what personality does for the individual, and at once inspires and co-ordinates all our thinking, so that it is the Spirit thinking in us. And then the thinkers themselves are hampered by an honourable concern lest in freely following and uttering their thought they should be committing their brethren, impairing *their* freedom, and forcing *their* consciences ; or lest they should be enjoying a position which is only given them by beliefs they renounce, and taking advantage of resources they obtained only by profession of what they now discard. It is impossible for thought to

act freely and beneficially under such conditions
as the absence of a creative foundation on the one
hand, and an inexpugnable footing of right on the
other. But were the Church to offer to its own
explorers as well as to the world a clear, brief,
and positive confession (evangelical and not theological, declared and not subscribed) of its one
creative Gospel whose nature is to quicken the
whole man and his thought, to quicken him to
life and not trim him to type—how much would
be gained for liberty! The precise form of such
a declaration would be matter of discussion. The
form offered by Dr. Denney might be taken; or
such a form as 2 Cor. v. 19, 21, if Scripture words
were desired; or such a version of it as that God
was in Christ forgiving and reconciling the world
by a new creation in the person and cross of Jesus
Christ, His only Son, our living Lord. Whatever
the form might be it would give the Church its true
moral basis and its only ground, firm amid the
swamps of sentiment and the blasts of criticism.
And it would not only allow but invite all critical
freedom that did not take the life of that generous
gospel which inspires the matter and passion of freedom. The two great departments of interest which
engross modern thought, and demand the re-casting
of much we inherit, are those that surround the
science of criticism on the one hand and the philosophy of immanence on the other. Both are Pro-

testant features, not to say products. And such a
declaration would give liberty and protection in the
Church to all competent criticism of the Bible or of
theology which did not dissolve the saving Christ;
and it would protect all the schooled philosophy of
immanence which did justice to the intimacy of
God in His world, but did not lose Him in a Monism
which is rather the absolutising of the immanent
than the incarnation of the transcendent.

In regard to Independency in particular, it may
be pointed out that, as the union of the free
churches becomes a more real thing, some such
share in a public statement of terms of communion may become a necessity. Otherwise Independency may be left behind, and relapse into
the isolated sectarianism against which its genius
has always protested; and it may do so, not for
the sake of the Gospel, but for the sake of an
unchartered freedom which it would then not draw
from the Gospel, but prefer to it.

And it may farther be remembered that the
valuable spiritualist tendencies whose timely ab-
sorption saved Independency for its great work at
the first will always be asserting themselves in a
communion so free; and they will always require
such a steadying and such a corrective as can be
given to Christians only by a rally upon their one
positive and creative base. A declaratory certainty

is, more even than liberty, not only the present need but the vital tradition and genius of the Independent Churches, for the sake both of their footing and their freedom.   And especially as they realise what was in their first stand.   Baillie, in his *Dissuasive from the Errors of the Time, and especially of the Independents,* says the independence of the congregation from presbytery or synod " was thought to be their proper distinctive and characteristical tenet, till of late we find them passionately reject the name Independents, and tell us that the dependency or independency of Congregationalism will be found to be one of their least differences and smallest controversies."   Independency was but a means to secure the better their great principle of evangelical prophetism, the free confession of a historic and individual salvation as a faith and not a theology.   It was, therefore, as the Presbyterians did not see, the trustee of things hidden or hated in the rest of Protestantism, those religious and social ideas, so rich for public life in Church and State, which, being rooted in the faith and inspiration of a positive gospel made the Reformation Dissenters the wellhead of future liberty and progress.   The polity, or ' apolity,' was there as a convenience for that gospel.   Its freedom was there only to serve that freedom.   It was not there for the sake of an abstract idea of liberty in ecclesiastical things, or to give scope to an unchartered

freedom. It was not even there to reproduce the
Church government of the New Testament. It
was there only for the sake of the positive liberty
that is in Christ, and in a Christ whose release of us
was evangelical or nothing. It was there to give
the utmost effect possible in Church and State to
something which was more precious than all the
liberty of the world because it was the source of it,
namely, the active will of God for the world's salvation through a forgiving redemption in the cross of
Jesus Christ. Independency stood for the Gospel
not as a limitation on liberty, but as its creative
source.

The more spiritual any historic movement is,
i.e. the more dependent on revelation, so much the
more it must return always to its classic source to
adjust its compass, and to realise its genius and its
call. And the more spiritual it is the more also it
will be found to have its classic and normative
time at its source. Its principle is in its creation,
like human freedom; which, being given by God,
was given for God. The more spiritual it is the
more is it of positive inspiration. And the inspiration of historic religions is chiefly with their founders
or their foundation. It is at their creative head.
The case is otherwise with movements which are
but evolutionary. There the process works up
from beneath instead of down from above. We

have then to do with a mere development and not
a revelation. So that we may find the law or
principle in the finished product more clearly and
powerfully than at the point of origin. And were
Christianity but the index instead of the cause of
man's spiritual evolution we should properly look
for its normative principle in the latest developments of the Christian conscience—if we did not
have to wait for it till the end of history. But
it is not so that we learn Christ. He is not a
great step in a greater process, not the hand at
the sluice which releases a greater power than it
possesses ; but He is Himself the fountainhead of
all that religion can ever be for man and his soul.
He is our freedom who is our new Creator. It is
to Him, therefore, and to the apostles He chose
and inspired for His self-revelation, that the Church
they created must always return for the standard,
as for the power, whereby it is to go on and
minister to each age as it arrives.

If it is so with the whole Church, it is so also
with each great movement within the Church itself
which recalls it to its true mission and genius. In
developing such movements we must, in proportion as they are spiritual, profound, and regal for
an age—we must return to their first spring, and
to the apostolic men in whom they rose to power
and effect. There we have the principle in its true
purity and force. There it was most deeply and

clearly grasped. It was bound to be so if it was to break through the frozen life, crusted prejudices, and iron orthodoxies round its source. The days of its creation are the days that contain the principle of its progress most richly, and mightily, and permanently. This was so in the Reformation. It is in the few first years of that renaissance of the new birth that we find its principle in its purity; when it flushed souls like a flame of fire in Luther, or a great smooth stream in Melanchthon; and before there resurged upon it the interests, the policies, and the scholasticisms which in a century had damped it to a smouldering mass, or clad it in a cumbrous mail.

And so it also is in the case of that Independency which, seizing and developing the core of the Reformation, seized and carried forward also, and still more purely, the principle of that gospel which the Reformation disentombed. It is to its Messiahs and apostles, not its forerunners, that we must recur for its true principle and gospel— not to its John Baptist, Robert Browne, not to the Anabaptist and ultra-spiritualistic tendencies which seethed with other elements in the cauldron of our first flux. But we go to those who disengaged the principle clearly and effectively from its alloys (so useful at a stage), and made it not only face but rule the hour in its true consciousness of itself. To Robinson, to Cromwell, to

Milton, to Goodwin, and their peers—it is to such
men, with a horizon and a lift in their thought,
that we must go—not to the dogmatists of a later
time, who burdened us with the debased Calvinism
of the eighteenth century, and who had lost the
great sense of our place in the whole Church and
the whole history of the founded freedom of the
West.   And when we so do, when we turn to these
classics, we shall find that our genius may perhaps
be fitly expressed in these two words that have
just fallen from my lips—FOUNDED FREEDOM.   Not
freedom alone is our genius ; for freedom alone is
but caprice, atomism, and anarchy in the end.
But it is freedom created and founded and reared
by an authority which cannot be either evaded or
shaken ; and which creates our emancipation, in the
very depth and crisis of our soul, by the eternal redemption at the heart of all history in Christ's cross.
It is our genius not simply to have set afloat on the
practical world the re-creative principle of freedom
and self-rule, political, social, and religious ; but
still more to have kept that principle in the closest
dependence on another, which is creative as God is,
and which is the principle of His new creation of us
in Jesus Christ.   It is to have preached and practised
the foundation of all liberty of thought or action,
public or private, in the evangelical freedom with
which Christ's cross makes free the world and the
soul.   That organic union of positivity and liberty of

Christian certainty and public freedom, in Church and State, is our genius and our trust. We have printed it on the free State; has our victory exhausted us of our power to commend it to a free Church? Are we too genial to be a power? more in love with liberty than sure of the one last condition which creates it? Are we amateurs of freedom rather than adepts of grace, a synagogue of the Libertines rather than a temple of the Holy Ghost?

We have a great tradition and a greater gospel. And the age has a great promise and a great need. It is a moral gospel and a moral need. They must meet in freedom. And we have much to do in the re-union.

Note to page 314.—Though if one were writing a complete estimate of Independency and its work, one would have to trace a considerable influence in the way of enlarging the independence of the single church within the great con- nectional bodies.